Faith-Based Organizations Emergency Planning Handbook

This document serves as a starting point for leaders of faith-based organizations to create a customized plan for their specific property and needs. Since every organization is different, the recommendations provided should be adapted accordingly. The author makes no guarantees about the completeness or effectiveness of your planning and accepts no responsibility for how this guidance is used.

Acknowledgment

Thank you to my lovely wife, Pam Briscoe, for her continuous and critical support throughout this entire process. I would also like to thank my family, Bryce, Essence, Kendrid, Connie, Justyce, Kyng, and Kayne for their daily blessings.

Finally, thanks to Justice Sakyi for her spiritual input and editing support.

Let's not forget Bowie State University, the flame of faith and the torch of truth.

Contents

Overview

A robust and actionable Emergency Plan (EP) is essential to protect the safety, survival, and well-being of all members and visitors. The foremost priority of every faith-based organization must be the preservation of life and the protection of God's house.

Church leadership should be prepared to respond to a variety of possible emergencies—including bomb threats, public health crises, active-shooter incidents, natural disasters, and even acts of terrorism. Effective preparation allows leaders to act swiftly, maintain order, and safeguard both people and property during unexpected events.

Every leader should keep a personal copy of the Emergency Plan and review it regularly. Whenever possible, staff and ministry members should also be familiar with its contents to ensure everyone understands their roles and responsibilities. Regular review and discussion of the plan help maintain readiness and confidence across the entire organization.

Purpose

The purpose of this handbook is to help faith-based leaders recognize and prepare for real-world threats that could impact the safety of members, students, and visitors during worship services, classes, and special events.

Our goal is to remove unnecessary distractions related to safety so that every person in attendance can focus fully on worship and fellowship with the Lord. Security exists not to instill fear but to create a secure and peaceful environment where faith can thrive.

Unfortunately, our communities have become increasingly affected by violence, crime, and hostility toward places of worship. The federal government has also acknowledged that both domestic and foreign extremist groups have expressed intent to target churches, schools, and other community gathering places.

While we pray for protection, we must also prepare wisely. As Scripture teaches, *"The prudent see danger and take refuge"* (Proverbs 27:12). Therefore, every congregation should be ready to respond confidently and effectively if ever faced with such threats.

The actions taken during the first few minutes of an emergency are often the most critical. A well-trained, well-informed response can mean the difference between chaos and calm—between harm and safety.

Quick and accurate communication saves lives. Prompt evacuation, sheltering, or lockdown procedures can protect those in danger. Immediate calls to emergency services ensure that first responders arrive with the right equipment and information. Trained members who can provide first aid or CPR may save lives while help is on the way.

Effective emergency planning requires that all leaders and staff understand their roles and responsibilities. Every person should know where to go, whom to contact, and what to do in a variety of situations. Familiarity with the facility—including exits, safe rooms, and emergency equipment—is vital.

Faith-based organizations should remember that preparation is both practical and spiritual. Planning reflects stewardship—caring for the people and property God has entrusted to us. Our goal is not fear but faith expressed through readiness, wisdom, and compassion.

"Be strong and of good courage, do not far nor be afraid of them; for the Lord your God, He is the One who goes with you. He will not leave you nor forsake you."

~Deuteronomy 31:6

Section 1: Risk Management

A sound approach to risk management helps faith-based organizations identify, evaluate, and reduce potential threats before they lead to harm or disruption. Risk management is both a practical and spiritual responsibility—an act of stewardship that protects God's people, property, and mission.

Types of Risk Management

1. Qualitative Risk Management

This approach uses expert judgment, experience, and observation to evaluate potential risks. Each risk is categorized—typically as *low, moderate,* or *high*—based on both the likelihood of occurrence and the potential impact. This method is often used when precise data is limited but practical knowledge and professional insight are available.

2. Quantitative Risk Management

This approach relies on numerical data and statistical analysis to determine the likelihood and impact of specific risks. It uses measurable values, models, and calculations to estimate probabilities and potential consequences in financial, environmental, or human terms. This method provides a more data-driven foundation for decision-making and prioritization.

Steps in Risk Management

1. Identification of Hazards

Identify all potential hazards or threats that could negatively affect your people, property, or operations. These may include natural disasters, acts of violence, health emergencies, equipment failures, or environmental issues.

2. Risk Analysis

Evaluate each identified hazard to determine how likely it is to occur and what the potential consequences would be. This step helps in understanding the magnitude and nature of each risk.

3. Risk Evaluation

Compare and rank the identified risks to determine which pose the greatest threat. Prioritize them based on severity and likelihood, focusing attention on the most critical areas first.

4. Risk Treatment

Develop and implement strategies to mitigate, manage, or eliminate identified risks. These strategies may include preventive measures, response plans, or partnerships with local emergency services.

5. Monitoring and Review

Regularly review and update your risk assessments to reflect new information, facility changes, or lessons learned from drills or real events. Continuous improvement ensures that your plan remains current and effective.

By following these steps, your organization builds resilience and readiness—prepared not only to respond to emergencies but also to prevent them when possible.

"The wise store up knowledge, but the mouth of a fool invites ruin."

- Proverbs 10:14

Risk Assessment

An effective risk assessment begins with identifying what could go wrong, analyzing how it might affect your organization, and developing strategies to minimize those impacts. This process helps faith-based leaders make wise, informed decisions to safeguard people, property, and ministry operations.

Importance of Risk Assessment

A thorough and ongoing risk assessment is essential for every faith-based organization. It allows leaders to anticipate potential dangers, make informed decisions, and strengthen the church's ability to respond effectively when challenges arise.

Risk assessment is not simply a technical exercise—it is an expression of wisdom and stewardship, demonstrating care for the people, property, and mission God has entrusted to us.

Proactive risk assessment reflects wisdom and foresight, enabling your church or ministry to protect lives, sustain operations, and demonstrate faithful stewardship of God's resources.

1. Proactive Risk Assessment

Conducting risk assessments enables your organization to identify and address potential threats before they escalate into full emergencies or crises. By anticipating what could go wrong, leaders can take proactive measures that prevent harm and ensure continuity of worship and ministry.

2. Decision Support

A well-documented risk assessment provides critical insight for decision-making. It highlights areas of greatest vulnerability, guiding leadership in allocating resources where they will have the most meaningful impact in reducing risk and enhancing safety.

3. Compliance and Regulation

Regular assessments also help ensure compliance with health, safety, and environmental laws. Following these standards not only protects your organization legally but also models integrity, accountability, and care for others.

By investing time in regular risk assessments, faith-based organizations strengthen their resilience, preparedness, and confidence. The result is a community better equipped to protect lives, maintain stability, and continue serving God faithfully—even in times of trial.

"The prudent see danger and take refuge, but the simple keep going and pay the penalty."

- Proverbs 27:12

Assessment Steps

1. Identifying Hazards

Begin by identifying all possible hazards that could impact your organization. These may include:

- **Natural disasters:** Hurricanes, tornadoes, floods, earthquakes, or severe storms.
- **Technological failures:** Power outages, network disruptions, or IT system breakdowns.
- **Human-related incidents:** Accidents, theft, security breaches, or acts of violence.
- **Environmental factors:** Pollution, hazardous materials, or climate-related events.

Each potential hazard should be carefully documented and evaluated for its potential to disrupt your ministry or endanger individuals.

2. Analyzing Hazard Scenarios

For every identified hazard, consider a range of possible scenarios—including different times, magnitudes, and locations. This process helps estimate both the likelihood of occurrence and the severity of potential impacts. Visualizing these scenarios allows leadership to prepare realistic, step-by-step responses.

3. Prioritizing Risks

Once potential hazards are identified, focus attention on those that pose the greatest threat to life, property, and continuity of ministry. Prioritization ensures resources and planning efforts address the most critical vulnerabilities first.

Key considerations include:

- Probability of occurrence
- Potential impact on people and property
- Disruption to essential operations or worship activities

4. Asset Assessment

Identify and evaluate your critical assets—those that must be protected or restored quickly after an emergency. This includes:

- **People:** Staff, volunteers, congregation members, and visitors.
- **Physical infrastructure:** Buildings, utilities, vehicles, and essential equipment.
- **Information technology:** Networks, data systems, and communication platforms.
- **Environmental resources:** Grounds, surrounding areas, and utilities that sustain operations.

Understanding which assets are vital helps guide risk mitigation, insurance planning, and resource allocation.

5. Vulnerability Analysis

Evaluate where your organization is most vulnerable to harm or disruption. Vulnerabilities may include weak building construction, insufficient security systems, inadequate emergency training, or outdated procedures. Recognizing these weaknesses allows you to take corrective actions—such as improving infrastructure, updating technology, or enhancing preparedness training.

Through careful identification, analysis, and prioritization, your organization can strengthen its resilience against potential threats. This approach reflects not only good management but also faithful stewardship, ensuring that your ministry remains strong and secure in service to God's people.

"By wisdom a house is built, and through understanding it is established."

- Proverbs 24:3

Impact Analysis

An effective Impact Analysis helps your organization understand how various disruptions could affect people, operations, and mission continuity. By identifying which processes are most essential and what losses would be most damaging, leaders can prioritize actions that protect both life and ministry.

1. Time-Sensitive or Critical Processes

Identify the key operations or ministries that are essential to the day-to-day functioning and mission of your organization. Evaluate the potential impact if these activities were disrupted—whether through power outages, data loss, facility damage, or other crises.

Examples may include:

- Worship services or ministry programs.
- Communication systems (phones, email, or live streaming).
- Financial management or donation tracking systems.

- Security, IT, or building operations.

Assess how long each process could be interrupted before it significantly harms your mission, reputation, or ability to serve.

2. Assessing Potential Impacts

Analyze the possible consequences of any major disruption. Consider how interruptions might affect:

- **Financial stability:** Loss of revenue, donations, or increased recovery costs.
- **Legal and regulatory obligations:** Compliance with safety, employment, or environmental laws.
- **Reputation and trust:** How delayed or poor responses could affect your community's confidence in leadership.
- **Service and outreach:** Missed ministry opportunities or inability to meet community needs.

Understanding these impacts allows leaders to prioritize protective measures and recovery strategies that ensure continuity of ministry and care for the congregation.

3. Importance of Prioritization

- **Human Safety First:**

Protecting life is always the top priority. Plans and procedures should first ensure the safety and well-being of every member, visitor, and staff member. Emergency training and clear communication can prevent injuries and save lives.

- **Protecting Assets and Operations:**

Next, safeguard the critical assets and resources that allow the organization to function. This includes facilities, technology, records, and finances. Continuity of operations supports the long-term stability of the ministry and prevents deeper disruptions.

- **Mitigating Environmental Impact:**

Consider how disasters or accidents might affect the surrounding environment. Ensure compliance with environmental regulations and take preventive measures to protect the local community and creation itself—a reflection of responsible stewardship of God's world.

By conducting a detailed Impact Analysis, leaders gain the insight needed to prepare, respond, and recover wisely. This process aligns with the biblical principle of foresight and diligence—caring for God's people and resources with both faith and prudence.

"Whatever you do, work at it with all your heart, as working for the Lord."

- Colossians 3:23

Mitigation and Preparedness

Mitigation and preparedness are the cornerstones of a resilient and faith-based organization. They involve taking proactive steps to reduce vulnerabilities, strengthen safety measures, and ensure that ministry operations can continue—even when challenges arise.

Importance of Mitigation

Mitigation plays a vital role in protecting the people, property, and mission of a faith-based organization. By acting before a disaster occurs, leaders demonstrate wisdom, foresight, and stewardship—fulfilling the biblical call to plan diligently and care for the resources entrusted to them.

1. Reducing Impact Severity

Effective mitigation efforts reduce the potential severity of harm from emergencies or disasters. Proactive steps such as reinforcing building structures, adding redundancy to critical systems, improving fire safety, and enhancing security measures can significantly limit damage and protect lives.

By planning and strengthening vulnerabilities, organizations create a safer environment for worship, ministry, and community service.

2. Cost Savings in the Long Run

Although mitigation requires an upfront investment, it often results in substantial long-term savings. Preventing damage, avoiding service disruptions, and minimizing recovery time are far less costly than responding to unplanned emergencies.

Preparedness not only protects finances but also safeguards the continuity of ministry, ensuring the church can continue to serve even in times of difficulty.

3. Enhancing Resilience

Mitigation strengthens an organization's ability to withstand and recover quickly from crises. A resilient church or ministry can adapt, respond effectively, and resume normal operations more quickly after an incident.

Resilience reflects both spiritual and practical readiness—combining faith in God's provision with disciplined planning.

"The wise store up choice food and olive oil, but fools gulp theirs down."

- Proverbs 21:20

By prioritizing mitigation, faith-based organizations not only protect their people and property but also uphold the biblical principle of stewardship—preparing wisely today to safeguard tomorrow.

Investing in mitigation now prevents greater losses later. It reduces the severity of potential impacts on people, property, and operations while saving time and resources during recovery.

Mitigation is not simply about defense—it's about faithful foresight. Proverbs 21:5 reminds us:

"The plans of the diligent lead surely to abundance, but everyone who is hasty comes only to poverty."

By thoughtfully preparing and maintaining strong controls, your organization honors both diligence and stewardship—protecting the ministry entrusted to your care.

Developing a Mitigation Strategy

Developing a strong mitigation strategy enables faith-based organizations to proactively reduce risks, protect lives, and ensure that ministry operations remain stable during times of crisis. A well-designed strategy transforms awareness into action—turning preparation into protection.

1. Identifying Mitigation Measures

Develop targeted actions to reduce or eliminate vulnerabilities revealed through assessment. These measures may include:

- **Engineering solutions:** Reinforcing building structures, installing fire suppression systems, or upgrading lighting and surveillance for security.
- **Operational improvements:** Strengthening emergency response protocols, training staff, or improving maintenance and safety inspections.

- **Policy and procedural updates:** Enforcing safety standards, enhancing reporting mechanisms, and ensuring compliance with local regulations.

Each action should be practical, achievable, and measurable, reflecting both good stewardship and sound leadership

2. Allocating Resources

Dedicate appropriate resources and funding to support your mitigation goals. Include costs for initial improvements, staff training, and long-term maintenance to sustain effectiveness over time.

Budgeting for safety is not an expense—it is an investment in the continued health and mission of your ministry. By planning financially for preparedness, the organization demonstrates responsible stewardship and foresight.

3. Engaging Stakeholders

Include key stakeholders in the planning and implementation process to ensure a broad understanding and shared commitment. This may involve staff, volunteers, congregation members, community partners, and local emergency authorities.

Collaborative engagement fosters unity and ensures that every participant understands their role in prevention and response. When the entire community is involved, preparedness becomes part of the organization's culture—not just a policy.

By following these steps, faith-based organizations can establish a strong mitigation framework that protects both people and purpose. Preparedness is an act of faith and diligence—a reflection of trust in God's sovereignty paired with wise and proactive stewardship.

"Plans fail for lack of counsel, but with many advisers they succeed."

- Proverbs 15:22

Types of Mitigation Measures

Mitigation involves taking intentional, proactive steps to reduce risks and minimize the impact of potential hazards. Effective mitigation strengthens both physical protection and community resilience—ensuring the safety, stability, and continued ministry of faith-based organizations.

1. Structural Improvements

Invest in building and infrastructure enhancements that increase the facility's ability to withstand natural and man-made hazards. Examples include:

- Reinforcing structures to resist earthquakes or high winds.
- Elevating or flood-proofing critical areas.
- Installing reliable power backup systems or surge protection.

These improvements not only safeguard property but also provide peace of mind, knowing the physical house of worship is well prepared to endure potential disasters.

2. Operational Changes

Enhance safety through organizational and procedural improvements. Examples include:

- Developing and maintaining detailed emergency response plans.
- Conducting regular training and drills for staff and volunteers.
- Strengthening internal and external communication systems.

Operational preparedness ensures that when emergencies occur, leaders and members can respond with clarity, coordination, and calm.

3. Natural Resource Management

Protect and preserve God's natural creation as part of a holistic mitigation strategy. Maintaining or restoring natural buffers such as wetlands, trees, and open green spaces to reduce the effects of floods, erosion, and extreme weather.

Caring for the environment is not only good risk management—it is also an act of stewardship, reflecting our responsibility to care for the earth wisely and sustainably.

4. Community Engagement and Education

Empower the congregation and local community through awareness, education, and collaboration. Provide workshops, training sessions, and informational materials that teach individuals how to prepare for and respond to emergencies.

Encourage a culture of shared responsibility where everyone contributes to safety and resilience. When knowledge is shared and faith is united, the entire community becomes stronger.

"My people are destroyed for lack of knowledge."

– Hosea 4:6

Implementing Controls

Develop and implement practical strategies to reduce risks before they escalate into emergencies. These may include:

- Strengthening building security and safety features.
- Establishing emergency response procedures and evacuation routes.
- Creating a continuity of operations plan to maintain essential ministry functions during a crisis.
- Training leaders, staff, and volunteers on their roles during emergencies.

Every measure implemented should align with your organization's mission and reflect a commitment to protecting God's people and resources with wisdom and care.

Regular Reviews and Updates

Preparedness is a continuous process. Conduct routine reviews and updates of your risk assessments, emergency plans, and mitigation strategies to ensure they remain current and effective.

Changes in the environment, facilities, technology, or congregation size can create new risks. Regularly evaluating and refining your plans ensures your organization stays ready for whatever challenges may come.

Continuous Improvement and Evaluation

Preparedness is not a one-time effort—it is a continuous process of growth and refinement. Regular evaluation ensures that your mitigation and preparedness strategies remain effective, relevant, and aligned with both current risks and your organization's mission.

Monitor Effectiveness

Regularly review and assess the effectiveness of all mitigation measures, emergency procedures, and training programs. Conduct after-action evaluations following drills or real incidents to identify what worked well and what can be improved.

Lessons learned from past experiences provide valuable insight, helping leadership refine plans and strengthen the organization's overall readiness.

By prioritizing mitigation and continuous improvement, faith-based organizations greatly reduce vulnerabilities and build lasting resilience. Each proactive step taken today strengthens the church's ability to protect lives, maintain ministry continuity, and serve as a beacon of hope during times of crisis.

"Teach us to number our days, that we may gain a heart of wisdom."
– Psalm 90:12

Section 2: Worship House Security Framework

Developing a Comprehensive Security Framework

A strong faith-based security plan involves a tiered and customized approach—addressing leadership, congregation, and perimeter security through proactive planning and collaboration.

Leadership Security

- **Risk Assessment:** Conduct detailed risk evaluations to identify vulnerabilities and threats to leaders.
- **Personal Security Measures:** Implement personalized safeguards such as secure transport, privacy controls, and protective oversight when necessary.

- **Communication Protocols:** Use secure communication systems for rapid response during emergencies.
- **Training and Awareness:** Equip leaders with the knowledge to recognize and respond to risks effectively.

Congregation Security

- **Observation and Monitoring:** Assign trained personnel to discreetly observe congregation activities.
- **Visitor Management:** Develop registration or greeting systems for newcomers.
- **Behavioral Awareness:** Train staff to identify unusual or potentially concerning behaviors.
- **Response Protocol:** Create response procedures that maintain safety without disrupting worship.

Perimeter Security

- **Physical Security Measures:** Establish clear boundaries using barriers, access controls, and surveillance systems.

- **Patrols and Vigilance:** Conduct routine checks inside and outside the facilities.
- **Visitor Oversight:** Monitor anyone loitering or acting suspiciously near the property.
- **Emergency Preparedness:** Develop response plans for threats such as unauthorized entry or suspicious packages.

Customized Approach

- **Tailored Plans:** Adapt all security measures to your church's size, structure, and community context.
- **Collaborative Efforts:** Foster teamwork among security personnel, ushers, and volunteers.
- **Continuous Evaluation:** Regularly review and improve procedures based on feedback and experience.

Training and Preparedness

- **Regular Training:** Provide ongoing instruction in awareness, de-escalation, and emergency response.

- **Drills and Exercises:** Practice real-world scenarios to test readiness.
- **Community Engagement:** Keep the congregation informed and involved in maintaining collective safety.

By adopting a tiered and adaptive framework, churches can uphold safety without compromising warmth or spiritual integrity. Collaboration, training, and vigilance—anchored in faith—form the foundation of lasting security.

Important Considerations for the Role of Church Security

The role of church security requires a unique balance of compassion, observation, and preparedness. Security team members serve as both protectors and ministers, ensuring safety while preserving the welcoming spirit of worship.

1. **Compassionate Service:**

The heart of church security lies in serving with compassion. This means caring for the congregation, responding with empathy, and reflecting Christ's love even during challenging circumstances.

2. **Observant and Vigilant:**

Security personnel must remain alert and proactive, continuously monitoring for potential risks while ensuring the well-being of members and guests.

3. **Strong Security Characteristics:**

A compassionate heart must be complemented by decisiveness, alertness, and readiness to act when necessary. Calm confidence and discernment are key.

4. **Understanding Limitations:**

Church security personnel should recognize their boundaries of authority. Unless legally certified, they must defer to law enforcement when situations exceed their training or jurisdiction.

5. **Contrast with Soldiers and Police:**

While military and law enforcement roles involve enforcement and confrontation, church security operates under a ministry framework—vigilant, disciplined, yet rooted in peace and de-escalation.

6. **Maintaining Public Order:**

Like law enforcement, church security promotes order—but within a faith-based, community-centered context, always upholding dignity, respect, and the church's values.

Summary:

Church security personnel play a critical role in protecting both people and purpose. They must be trained, compassionate, aware of their limitations, and prepared to collaborate with local authorities when needed. Through this balanced approach, they help maintain a safe, welcoming, and spiritually grounded environment for worship and fellowship.

Developing a Robust Emergency Plan (EP)

Developing a comprehensive and executable Emergency Plan (EP) is essential for protecting the lives and well-being of members, staff, and visitors during any form of crisis or disruption. A well-prepared plan provides guidance, structure, and confidence in moments when clarity matters most.

Below is a structured, faith-aligned approach to creating and implementing an effective EP:

1. Assessment and Planning

- **Identify Potential Risks:** Conduct a thorough risk assessment to recognize the types of emergencies your organization might face—such as natural disasters, medical incidents, or security threats.
- **Establish an Emergency Response Team:** Appoint dedicated individuals responsible for implementing and coordinating all emergency procedures. Each member should understand their specific duties and chain of command.

2. Plan Development

- **Define Roles and Responsibilities:** Clearly assign duties to each team member to ensure accountability and coordination during emergencies.
- **Create Response Procedures:** Develop step-by-step procedures for a variety of potential incidents—including

evacuation routes, lockdown instructions, medical responses, and communication protocols.

- **Consider Special Needs:** Account for members or visitors with disabilities, language barriers, or medical conditions that may require additional assistance during emergencies.

3. Communications

- **Internal Communication:** Establish a clear system for quickly notifying leaders, staff, and congregation members when emergencies arise.
- **External Communication:** Develop guidelines for communicating with emergency services, local authorities, media outlets, and neighboring organizations during crises.

4. Training and Drills

- **Training Sessions:** Conduct regular training for all staff and volunteers so they understand their emergency roles, procedures, and safe responses.
- **Mock Drills:** Schedule routine drills to test the effectiveness of your plan, evaluate readiness, and strengthen coordination among all participants.

5. Resource Management

- **Allocate Resources:** Maintain an inventory of essential emergency supplies such as first aid kits, radios, flashlights, and bottled water.
- **Build Partnerships:** Partner with local emergency responders, neighboring churches, and community organizations to provide mutual aid when needed.

6. Plan Review and Updates

- **Regular Reviews:** Evaluate and update the plan periodically, incorporating lessons learned from drills, incidents, and feedback from staff and members.
- **Ensure Accessibility:** Keep printed and digital copies of the most recent plan accessible to all leaders and staff involved in emergency response.

7. Crisis Response

- **Immediate Activation:** When an emergency occurs, activate the plan immediately to ensure a rapid, coordinated, and organized response.

- **Post-Incident Assessment:** After the situation is resolved, hold a debriefing session to evaluate what worked well and what could be improved for future readiness.

8. Cultural Adoption

- **Foster a Culture of Safety:** Encourage all staff and members to view preparedness as a shared responsibility. Emphasize that readiness honors God's call to stewardship and care for others.

- **Promote Continuous Learning:** Make emergency preparedness an ongoing part of organizational culture through education, prayer, and regular communication.

By following these structured steps, your organization can build a living plan—one that not only strengthens physical safety but also reinforces faith, unity, and resilience. Consistent review, training, and teamwork will help ensure readiness and peace of mind for every member of your community.

Priority Protective Actions for Life Safety

In any emergency, the **number one priority is the protection of life**. Effective preparation and immediate, coordinated action can greatly reduce harm and ensure safety for all members, staff, and visitors.

By prioritizing these protective measures, your organization builds a culture of readiness and calm confidence during critical situations. Preparation ensures that when emergencies arise, the congregation responds with clarity, unity, and faith instead of fear.

"Let all things be done decently and in order."

– 1 Corinthians 14:40

Below are the key protective actions every faith-based organization should plan, practice, and review regularly:

Protective Actions for Life Safety

A church's preparedness extends beyond prevention; it includes effective response and recovery during emergencies.

Protective actions such as evacuation, shelter-in-place, lockdown procedures, and earthquake preparedness are essential for safeguarding lives in various scenarios. Each plan should be clearly communicated, rehearsed, and supported by every ministry team.

Faith-based organizations must prepare for a variety of emergencies—ranging from natural disasters to security incidents.

The following protective actions outline how to respond swiftly, calmly, and effectively, preserving safety while maintaining order and compassion.

1. Life Safety Basics

- **Stay Informed:**

Stay updated through emergency alerts, radio, or mobile notification systems. Follow all instructions issued by local authorities or emergency services.

- **Seek Shelter:**

Move quickly to a safe location away from hazards such as fire, flooding, or violent threats. Always prioritize safety over property.

- **Administer First Aid:**

If trained, provide immediate first aid to those who are injured while awaiting emergency medical assistance.

- **Communicate:**

When possible, use phones or radios to communicate your location, condition, and needs to emergency personnel or leadership.

2. Evacuation Procedures

- **Respond to Alarms:**

Treat every fire alarm or evacuation order as real. Act immediately and calmly.

- **Stay Calm:**

Maintain composure and help others remain calm. Your demeanor can prevent panic and confusion.

- **Follow Exit Signs:**

Use the nearest safe exit route, following illuminated exit signs. Avoid elevators during emergencies.

- **Assist Others:**

Offer help to elderly, disabled, or young individuals who may require assistance evacuating.

- **Bring Essentials:**

If time permits, take essential items such as medications, identification, and emergency supplies.

- **Test Fire Alarms:**

Conduct regular alarm tests as required by local regulations. Notify occupants in advance and observe response times to ensure procedures are understood.

- **Maintain Exits:**

Inspect all exit routes frequently to ensure they are unobstructed, properly marked, and code-compliant.

- **Reach a Safe Place:**

Assemble at a designated meeting area outside the building. Account for all individuals and remain there until cleared by emergency personnel.

3. Sheltering / Shelter-in-Place

Sheltering in place means remaining inside a safe location when external hazards make evacuation unsafe. This is used for events such as severe weather, hazardous materials, or external security threats.

Steps for Sheltering in Place:

1. **Receive Notification:**

Act promptly upon hearing an official alert or instruction to shelter in place.

2. Select a Safe Location:

Choose an interior room with no windows, preferably on a lower floor (e.g., a hallway, classroom, or storage room).

3. Seal the Shelter Area:

Close and, if necessary, seal windows, vents, and doors using plastic sheeting and duct tape to block contaminants.

4. Turn Off HVAC Systems:

Shut down heating and air conditioning systems to prevent contaminated air from entering.

5. Monitor Emergency Alerts:

Stay tuned to radio, TV, or mobile alerts for situation updates and all-clear notices.

6. Prepare Emergency Supplies:

Keep a ready kit with water, non-perishable food, a flashlight, a radio, batteries, and basic medical supplies.

7. Communicate and Stay Calm:

Reassure others, maintain a calm environment, and communicate with authorities when safe to do so.

8. **Follow Official Instructions:**

Remain sheltered until emergency officials declare it safe to exit.

Additional Tips:

- Practice shelter-in-place drills regularly.
- Keep emergency contact lists accessible.
- Remain patient—events requiring sheltering can last several hours.

4. Lockdown Procedures

Lockdown procedures protect occupants from immediate threats such as intruders or active shooters. The goal is to secure and conceal until law enforcement arrives.

Steps for Lockdown:

- **Secure Your Location:**

  Immediately lock or barricade all doors and block entry points using available furniture or equipment.

- **Stay Quiet and Hidden:**

Silence phones, turn off lights, and remain out of sight and away from windows.

- **Follow Instructions:**

  Cooperate fully with law enforcement or security personnel once they arrive. Do not open doors until given an all-clear by identifiable officials.

- **Communicate Quietly:**

  Use silent communication methods such as text messaging to notify authorities of your location and any information about the threat.

- **Assist Others:**

  Help those nearby stay calm, remain hidden, and follow lockdown procedures.

- **Stay Alert:**

  Remain vigilant until the all-clear is issued; secondary threats may still exist.

5. Earthquake Preparedness

Earthquake readiness saves lives by minimizing injury during sudden shaking.

- **Drop, Cover, and Hold On:**

Drop to your hands and knees, take cover under a sturdy object, and hold on until the shaking stops.

- **Stay Indoors:**

If inside, remain indoors — move away from windows, glass, or heavy objects that could fall.

- **Evacuate if Unsafe:**

After shaking stops, assess for damage. If the structure is unsafe, evacuate calmly. In coastal regions, follow tsunami evacuation procedures if applicable.

- **Prepare Emergency Kits:**

Keep earthquake survival kits readily available with water, food, flashlights, radios, and first aid supplies.

Training, Drills, and Compliance

1. Regular drills and rehearsals are essential. Ensure all staff and volunteers:
2. Understand evacuation and sheltering routes.
3. Are familiar with emergency assembly points.
4. Participate in quarterly or semiannual safety drills.

5. Comply with all local fire and building safety codes.

"God is our refuge and strength, an ever-present help in trouble."

~ Psalm 46:1

Additional Tips

- **Know Your Surroundings:**

  Familiarize yourself with building layouts, exits, and potential shelter locations.

- **Practice Lockdown Drills:**

  Participate regularly in lockdown exercises to build confidence and readiness.

- **Communicate Responsibly:**

  During an incident, avoid spreading rumors or sharing unverified information.

- **Cooperate with Authorities:**

  When law enforcement arrives, follow all instructions promptly and calmly. Keep hands visible at all times.

- Evacuation: Move everyone safely and calmly out of the building to a designated assembly area or safe location, following pre-identified evacuation routes

"The Lord is my light and my salvation – whom shall I fear? The Lord is the stronghold of my life – of whom shall I be afraid?"

~ Psalm 27:1

The Unique Role and Responsibilities of Church and Faith-Based Organizations Security

Those who serve in church security ministries play a vital and sacred role: to protect God's people, create an atmosphere of peace, and ensure that worship and learning occur without fear.

Security ministry is not about control—it is about care, vigilance, and stewardship. It requires both practical readiness and spiritual discernment. Team members must balance situational awareness with compassion, acting as guardians who protect while maintaining the welcoming spirit of the ministry.

Key principles include:

- Service through protection: Safeguarding others as an act of ministry and love.
- Calm leadership: Responding to tension or threat with composure and faith.
- Training and discipline: Regularly preparing for various scenarios to ensure confidence and coordination.
- Partnership: Working closely with church leadership, local law enforcement, and the congregation to maintain a unified safety culture.

Ultimately, those who serve in this capacity embody Jesus' call to shepherd His people—standing ready, alert, and faithful in both heart and action.

"Be on your guard; stand firm in the faith; be courageous; be strong."

– 1 Corinthians 16:13

Characteristics of a Church Security Team Member

Serving on a Church Security Team is both a privilege and a calling. Members are entrusted with the sacred responsibility of protecting God's people while maintaining the atmosphere of love, peace, and welcome that defines the body of Christ.

Security service in the church is ministry first, mission always—blending compassion with vigilance to ensure that every worshipper can experience God's presence without fear.

1. Compassionate Heart

The foundation of all church security work is compassion. A team member's primary mission is to serve others selflessly, ensuring their safety and peace of mind during worship, study, and fellowship.

Compassion in security means greeting people warmly, responding to needs with kindness, and showing patience even in stressful moments. Security is not about authority – it's about care, expressed through calm presence and protective service.

"Be kind and compassionate to one another, forgiving each other, just as in Christ God forgave you."

- Ephesians 4:32

2. Observant and Alert

A successful church security member is both vigilant and aware. They continually observe their surroundings, noticing details that others might overlook – from unattended bags to changes in behavior or mood that may signal distress.

Being observant is not about suspicion; it's about discernment – seeing with both natural awareness and spiritual insight. Through attentiveness, security members can identify and address potential issues before they become emergencies.

"Be alert and of sober mind. Your enemy the devil prowls around like a roaring lion looking for someone to devour."

- 1 Peter 5:8

3. Strong Security Traits

While maintaining a compassionate and faith-filled approach, church security members must also develop strong professional traits that enable effective responses in critical situations. These include:

- **Attentiveness:** Remaining focused and engaged throughout services or events.
- **Readiness:** Being mentally and physically prepared to respond quickly when needed.
- **Calm under pressure:** Acting with composure and clear judgment during stressful or emergency situations.
- **Discipline:** Following established protocols and communicating clearly within the team structure.

Such qualities build confidence among both the congregation and the team itself, ensuring that safety is maintained without disrupting the spirit of worship.

"The prudent see danger and take refuge, but the simple keep going and pay the penalty."

- Proverbs 27:12

Together, these characteristics form the heart of an effective church security ministry—one that reflects both the love of Christ and the wisdom of preparedness. A compassionate, alert, and disciplined team not only safeguards the congregation but also strengthens the church's witness as a place of peace, order, and trust.

Church and Faith-Based Security Ministry: Roles and Responsibilities

Serving in a security ministry within a church or faith-based school is a sacred calling. Those who stand watch do so not out of fear but out of love—ensuring that all who come to worship, learn, or serve do so in peace and safety. Security personnel are servants and stewards, protecting the congregation and staff as an act of ministry.

As Nehemiah organized watchmen over Jerusalem's walls (Nehemiah 7:3), modern-day protectors stand as faithful guardians of God's house—alert, disciplined, and guided by His wisdom.

1. Mission and Purpose of the Security Ministry

- Provide a safe, welcoming, and orderly environment for worship, education, and community gatherings.

- Protect members, students, staff, and visitors from potential harm or disruption.
- Respond swiftly and appropriately to emergencies, medical incidents, or security threats.
- Support leadership in maintaining calm and confidence during critical situations.

Security is not meant to intimidate; it is meant to reassure and enable worship. When people feel safe, they can focus fully on spiritual growth and fellowship.

2. Spiritual Foundation of Security Service

Security work is more than a procedure. It is ministry in motion.

- Team members must approach their role with humility, vigilance, and prayer.
- Each act of observation, intervention, or assistance should be rooted in compassion and guided by the Holy Spirit.
- Servants of security reflect God's own nature as protector and shepherd (Psalm 121:7-8).

"The Lord will keep you from all harm — He will watch over your life; the Lord will watch over your coming and going both now and forevermore."

- Psalm 121:7-8

3. Core Responsibilities

Security ministry responsibilities extend beyond guarding doors; they encompass prevention, readiness, and care.

a. Prevention and Presence

- Maintain a visible yet welcoming presence before, during, and after services or school hours.
- Observe unusual behavior, unattended items, or potential hazards.
- Greet and assist attendees in a friendly manner to create comfort and deter wrongdoing.

b. Emergency Response

- Respond immediately to incidents such as medical emergencies, suspicious activity, or disturbances.
- Follow established emergency plans for evacuation, lockdown, or shelter-in-place as appropriate.

- Coordinate with ministry leaders and emergency responders while ensuring calm communication with the congregation.

c. Communication and Coordination

- Maintain reliable communication (radios, phones) among team members and leadership.
- Ensure clarity in reporting incidents, following the chain of command, and documenting events accurately.

d. Training and Professionalism

- Participate in regular training sessions, drills, and scenario-based exercises.
- Stay familiar with emergency procedures, local laws, and first-aid protocols.
- Model integrity, discretion, and respect in all interactions.

4. Collaboration with Law Enforcement and Community Partners

Establish strong partnerships with local law enforcement, fire departments, and emergency medical services. Joint collaboration enhances response coordination and strengthens the ministry's credibility.

Security leaders should:

- Share emergency plans and facility maps with first responders.
- Participate in local safety meetings or community preparedness programs.
- Invite law enforcement to assist with training and threat-awareness education.

"Two are better than one, because they have a good return for their labor: if either of them falls down, one can help the other up."

– Ecclesiastes 4:9-10

5. Ethics, Confidentiality, and Compassion

Security ministry members must act with the highest ethical and spiritual integrity.

- Protect privacy and confidentiality regarding incidents or individuals.
- Treat every person — even those causing disruption — with dignity and grace.
- Balance enforcement with empathy, ensuring that every response honors Christ's example of truth and love.

6. Continuous Development and Spiritual Growth

Security ministry members should commit to ongoing learning and spiritual maturity.

- Attend periodic training in safety, crisis management, and de-escalation techniques.
- Engage in prayer, devotion, and team fellowship to stay spiritually grounded.
- Reflect on each experience as an opportunity to grow in wisdom and service.

"Watch, stand fast in the faith, be brave, be strong. Let all that you do be done with love."

– 1 Corinthians 16:13-14

7. Leadership and Accountability

Security ministry leaders must provide clear direction, mentorship, and accountability. They should ensure all volunteers are properly vetted, trained, and spiritually prepared. Leadership includes:

- Defining the team structure and responsibilities.
- Conducting background checks and maintaining confidentiality.

- Promoting unity, discipline, and open communication within the team.

Strong leadership fosters trust and ensures the ministry operates with excellence and grace.

Conclusion

The church and faith-based ministry stands as a shield of protection and a beacon of calm. Its purpose is not rooted in fear but in faith—to safeguard the body of Christ and create a sanctuary of peace.

Through prayer, preparation, and presence, security volunteers serve as extensions of God's care, embodying both vigilance and compassion in every action.

"Blessed be the Lord, my rock, who trains my hands for war, and my fingers for battle."

- Psalm 144:1

Role Limitations and Guidelines

1. Conflict Resolution

Church security personnel who are not part of law enforcement should refrain from intervening in conflicts that require official legal authority.

They must understand the boundaries of their role and promptly seek assistance from law enforcement when situations exceed their responsibility or training.

2. Avoiding Aggressive Tactics

Unlike soldiers or law enforcement officers trained for combat or direct confrontation, church security members should maintain a calm, controlled, and non-aggressive posture.

Their approach should always reflect the values of compassion, safety, and peace within the church environment.

3. Understanding Authority

Distinction from Police Officers

Church security personnel do not possess the same legal authority as sworn law enforcement officers.

Their primary responsibility is to help maintain order, safety, and a welcoming atmosphere within the church.

In situations involving potential legal violations or criminal activity, they must immediately defer to and cooperate with law enforcement authorities.

Balancing Security and Compassion

Preventive Measures

Focus on proactive security strategies that prioritize prevention over confrontation. This includes maintaining effective access control, ensuring comprehensive emergency preparedness, and building strong relationships with local law enforcement for coordinated response and support.

Communication and Training

Hold regular meetings, communication briefings, and training sessions to ensure that all security team members clearly understand their roles, responsibilities, and limitations. Ongoing education reinforces both operational readiness and a compassionate approach aligned with the church's mission and values.

"Be on your guard; stand firm in the faith; be courageous; be strong. Do everything in love."

~1 Corinthians 16:13-14

Collaborative Approach

Teamwork and Coordination

Foster strong collaboration among church staff, volunteers, and security personnel to build a unified approach to safety.

When all members work together guided by clear communication and shared responsibility, the church becomes a secure and welcoming environment for worship, fellowship, and community activities.

By emphasizing compassion, attentiveness, and a clear understanding of roles and limitations, church security teams can effectively contribute to the protection and peace of the congregation while maintaining a respectful and non-confrontational atmosphere.

"Two are better than one, because they have a good return for their labor: If either of them falls down, one can help the other up."

~ *Ecclesiastes 4:9–10*

Developing a comprehensive security framework for faith-based organizations involves addressing the unique needs of leadership, the congregation, and the facility perimeter. The following section will outline specific strategies for strengthening security in each of these areas.

Leadership Security Procedures

1. **Personal Security Measures**

- Establish clear security protocols for church and organizational leaders.

- Conduct periodic threat assessments to identify potential risks and implement appropriate safeguards.
- Maintain secure communication channels for sensitive discussions and confidential information.
- When necessary, coordinate personal protection measures to ensure the safety and well-being of leadership during services, events, or travel.

2. Access Control

- Implement controlled access procedures to leadership offices or restricted areas.
- Utilize sign-in protocols, key cards, or designated escorts to prevent unauthorized individuals from approaching leaders without clearance.
- Ensure that staff and volunteers understand access boundaries and maintain discretion regarding leadership schedules or movements.

"I said to them, 'Do not open the gates of Jerusalem until the sun is hot, and while the gatekeepers are still on duty, have them shut the doors and bar them."

~ Nehemiah 7:3

Congregation Security During Services

1. **Observation and Monitoring**

Designate trained security personnel to remain attentive during all worship services and church activities.

Maintain situational awareness by observing the congregation for any unusual behavior, potential disruptions, or emerging security threats.

Ensure monitoring is conducted with discretion and respect, preserving the reverent and welcoming atmosphere of worship.

2. **Visitor Management**

Extend a warm and welcoming attitude toward new visitors while maintaining alertness to any concerning behavior or irregular patterns.

Coordinate with ushers and greeters to ensure visitors are greeted, guided appropriately, and integrated safely into the service environment.

Keep a clear balance between hospitality and vigilance, ensuring the church remains both open and secure.

3. **Response to Suspicious Activity**

Provide security team members with training and protocols for responding calmly and appropriately to unusual, disruptive, or threatening behavior.

Responses should prioritize de-escalation, safety, and discretion, avoiding confrontation whenever possible.

In the event of an immediate threat, security personnel should act swiftly to protect the congregation and contact law enforcement as needed.

"Be alert and of sober mind. Your enemy the devil prowls around like a roaring lion looking for someone to devour."

~ 1 Peter 5:8

Facility and Perimeter Security

1. Physical Security Measures

- Secure both the interior and exterior perimeters of the church facility using appropriate safety measures such as physical barriers, access controls, and surveillance systems.
- Ensure that entrances, exits, and parking areas are well-lit and monitored to deter unauthorized access and suspicious activity.

- Conduct regular inspections of locks, alarms, and cameras to confirm that all security equipment is functioning properly.
- Encourage coordination between church staff and local law enforcement to strengthen overall facility protection.

2. Monitoring Common Areas

- Assign security personnel or trained volunteers to monitor hallways, lobbies, classrooms, and gathering spaces during services and events.
- Address concerns such as young members or visitors repeatedly walking through restricted or unsupervised areas to maintain order and prevent potential disruptions.
- Ensure that all interactions remain respectful, calm, and discreet, preserving the sense of hospitality and reverence within the church environment.

"Unless the Lord watches over the city, the guards stand watch in vain."

~ Psalm 127:1

Transition: Perimeter Security Options

A secure church environment extends beyond the sanctuary. Perimeter security elements—including proper lighting, thoughtful landscaping, a visible security presence, and modern surveillance systems—play a vital role in deterring potential threats and ensuring the safety and comfort of members and visitors alike. The following section provides a detailed breakdown of these essential components.

1. Lighting

- **Importance of Proper Lighting**

- Adequate lighting is one of the most effective deterrents against criminal activity and safety hazards. Ensure that key areas such as parking lots, walkways, entrances, and exits are well-lit to promote visibility, discourage suspicious behavior, and help members feel safe when arriving or leaving services.

- **Risk Assessment**

Incorporate lighting evaluations into your overall security risk assessment. Identify dimly lit areas, blind spots, or locations with inconsistent lighting that may increase vulnerability. Adjust or install additional lighting where needed to achieve uniform coverage and improve nighttime safety.

- **Types of Lighting**
- Utilize bright, energy-efficient lighting—such as LED fixtures—that provide clear illumination without glare or harsh shadows. Avoid overly bright lighting that can create contrast issues; instead, aim for balanced visibility that supports both security and comfort. Consider motion-activated or timed lighting systems for efficiency and after-hours protection.

"You, Lord, keep my lamp burning; my God turns my darkness into light."

~ Psalm 18:28

2. Landscaping

- Smart Landscaping Practices:
- Maintain landscaping with intentional design to support both beauty and safety. Regularly trim shrubs, trees, and hedges to prevent overgrowth that could obstruct visibility, provide hiding places, or create unease among members and visitors. A well-kept exterior communicates

care, order, and attentiveness—qualities that reflect the church's stewardship of its environment.

- Clear Lines of Sight:
- Ensure that all security cameras, entry points, and walkways have clear lines of sight by trimming vegetation and maintaining open spaces. Strategic landscaping improves natural surveillance, allowing staff, volunteers, and security personnel to detect and respond quickly to potential concerns. Balance security with aesthetics by choosing low-maintenance plants and open designs that enhance visibility without diminishing the church's welcoming appearance.

"For God is not a God of disorder but of peace – as in all the congregations of the Lord's people."

~1 Corinthians 14:33

3. Visible Security Presence

Deterrence and Reassurance

A visible security presence serves two vital purposes. It deters potential threats and reassures the congregation that their safety is a priority. Trained and approachable security personnel stationed at key areas such as entrances, parking lots, and hallways create a calm, confident atmosphere that promotes both safety and peace of mind.

Professionalism and Conduct

Security personnel should reflect the values of the church through their demeanor and communication. They should remain attentive yet approachable, demonstrating courtesy, discretion, and respect in every interaction. Their conduct should reassure visitors that safety and hospitality coexist harmoniously within the church environment.

Engagement and Support

Encourage security team members to build positive relationships with the congregation. Familiarity fosters trust and cooperation, allowing members to feel comfortable reporting concerns. A visible presence should never feel intimidating but instead serve as a quiet ministry of protection, care, and service.

"The Lord will keep you from all harm – he will watch over your life; the Lord will watch over your coming and going both now and forevermore."

Psalm 121:7–8

4. Security Cameras and Surveillance Systems

Strategic Placement:

Install security cameras in key areas such as entrances, parking lots, hallways, and other high-traffic or vulnerable zones. Proper camera placement enhances visibility, supports incident response, and provides valuable documentation in case of security events. Position cameras to cover blind spots while maintaining the privacy and comfort of worshippers.

Monitoring and Maintenance:

Establish consistent monitoring procedures during services and events to ensure timely awareness of unusual activities. Regularly inspect and maintain all cameras, recording systems, and storage devices to verify they are operational and producing clear footage. A reliable surveillance system supports both prevention and post-incident analysis.

Privacy and Ethical Use:

Use surveillance responsibly, with respect for the privacy and dignity of all congregants. Avoid intrusive or excessive monitoring in worship areas and private spaces. Clearly communicate the purpose of camera use—to protect, not to invade—and ensure that all data is handled securely and confidentially.

"Do not forsake wisdom, and she will protect you; love her, and she will watch over you."

~ ***Proverbs 4:6***

Focus on Safety and Hospitality

- Balancing Security with a Welcoming Atmosphere

  Strive to maintain a thoughtful balance between effective security measures and the warm, inclusive spirit that defines your faith community. While vigilance is essential, the church should always remain a place of peace, compassion, and open fellowship. Security procedures should enhance—not hinder—the worship experience.

- Communication and Preparedness

  Encourage open communication channels between leadership, security personnel, and congregation members. Transparency builds trust and ensures that potential concerns are identified early. Regular drills, updates, and meetings promote collective preparedness, helping everyone feel confident and secure during services and events.

By approaching security from a tiered perspective—addressing the needs of leadership, congregation, and facility perimeter—faith-based organizations can create a secure environment that fosters worship, fellowship, and community engagement. A well-balanced security plan promotes peace of mind while reflecting the church's mission of care and stewardship.

"May there be peace within your walls and security within your citadels."

~ Psalm 122:7

Integration and Holistic Approach

Comprehensive Security Strategy:

Combine all physical and procedural elements—lighting, landscaping, visible security presence, and surveillance technology—into a unified, comprehensive security strategy. Each measure should complement the others to create a layered and balanced approach that addresses the specific risks, size, and environment of the faith-based organization. An integrated plan ensures both prevention and preparedness while maintaining the church's mission of peace and community care.

Community Engagement:

Encourage active participation and communication among congregation members regarding security awareness. Open discussions foster understanding, cooperation, and trust, allowing everyone to share responsibility for maintaining a safe and welcoming place of worship. When the entire congregation is informed and engaged, security becomes a shared ministry of stewardship and compassion.

By integrating these perimeter security options within a broader, holistic framework, faith-based organizations can strengthen overall safety, deter potential threats, and cultivate an environment where worship and fellowship flourish. A well-balanced approach not only protects people and property but also reinforces the church's role as a beacon of peace, trust, and spiritual refuge.

"My people will live in peaceful dwelling places, in secure homes, in undisturbed places of rest."

~ Isaiah 32:18

Section 3: Key Principles of Secure Leadership

Leadership Training and Preparedness

- **Commit to Continuous Training:**

  Provide regular leadership and response training for pastors, ministry staff, and security teams to enhance preparedness and confidence in crisis situations.

  Conduct scheduled drills and tabletop exercises to test communication systems, evacuation procedures, and coordination among response partners.

- **Foster a Culture of Readiness:**

  Promote a spirit of vigilance and stewardship—recognizing that preparedness is a form of service and care for the congregation.

  Encourage all leaders to remain spiritually grounded and mentally ready to act with wisdom and courage when emergencies arise.

"Be strong and courageous... for the Lord your God will be with you wherever you go." –

~ ***Joshua 1:9***

Empowerment and Trust

- **Decision-Making Empowerment:**

Effective and secure leaders empower their team members by offering guidance, training, and clear expectations while allowing room for sound judgment and initiative. When team members are trusted to make decisions within established protocols, they develop confidence, accountability, and ownership in fulfilling their responsibilities. Empowered teams operate more effectively under pressure and respond more cohesively during critical situations.

- **Trust and Accountability:**

Building a culture of trust strengthens unity and reliability within the security team. When leaders demonstrate faith in their members' abilities, it fosters an environment of mutual respect and commitment. Trust naturally leads to accountability, as individuals take pride in their service and understand the importance of their role in protecting and supporting the congregation's mission.

"As iron sharpens iron, so one person sharpens another."

~ Proverbs 27:17

Synergy and Collaboration

Encouraging Synergy:

Secure leaders recognize that the strength of a team lies in its unity and diversity. By encouraging members to collaborate, share insights, and develop solutions together, leaders foster synergy that enhances creativity, efficiency, and mutual respect. Empowering individuals to contribute their unique skills and perspectives allows the team to operate harmoniously and respond more effectively to challenges.

Defined Expectations:

Clear goals and expectations provide direction while leaving room for innovation. When team members understand the mission, objectives, and desired outcomes, they can coordinate efforts confidently and purposefully. Defined expectations ensure accountability, while collaborative freedom inspires initiative and strengthens the team's collective performance.

"Two are better than one, because they have a good return for their labor: If either of them falls down, one can help the other up."

~ Ecclesiastes 4:9–10

Growth and Development

Challenge for Growth:

Secure leaders understand that growth occurs when individuals are encouraged to think critically, innovate, and step beyond their comfort zones. By presenting new challenges and opportunities for development, leaders cultivate stronger, more resilient team members who adapt with confidence and purpose. Encouraging creative problem-solving strengthens both personal capability and the team's overall effectiveness.

Belief in Team Members:

Demonstrating genuine belief in the abilities and potential of each team member builds confidence and motivation. When leaders express trust, support, and recognition, individuals feel valued and empowered to reach higher levels of performance and service. A leader's faith in their team not only fosters excellence but also reflects Christlike encouragement and stewardship of each person's unique gifts.

"I can do all this through him who gives me strength."

~ Philippians 4:13

Support and Recognition:

- Removing Obstacles:

Secure leaders take a servant-leadership approach, focusing on removing barriers and providing the tools, resources, and guidance necessary for their team to succeed. By identifying challenges and addressing them proactively, leaders create an environment where team members can focus on their mission with confidence and clarity. A supportive leader enables others to perform their roles effectively and grow in both skill and faith.

- Giving Credit and Taking Responsibility:

True leadership is marked by humility and accountability. Secure leaders celebrate the accomplishments of their team, giving recognition where it is due and uplifting others' contributions. At the same time, they take responsibility when challenges arise, modeling integrity and grace under pressure. This approach builds trust, strengthens unity, and nurtures a culture of gratitude, respect, and collaboration within the organization.

"Do nothing out of selfish ambition or vain conceit. Rather, in humility value others above yourselves, not looking to your own interests but each of you to the interests of the others."

~ ***Philippians 2:3–4***

Passion and Inspiration

- **Motivating Action:**

Secure leaders inspire their teams through genuine passion and enthusiasm for the mission they serve. Their energy, dedication, and positive example motivate others to act with purpose and conviction. When leaders model commitment and faith-driven motivation, they create a ripple effect—empowering team members to embrace their roles with joy, diligence, and spiritual confidence.

- Encouraging Innovation:

Great leaders challenge complacency and encourage creative thinking. By promoting a culture where it is safe to question the status quo and explore new approaches, they cultivate continuous improvement and adaptability. Encouraging innovation ensures the team remains effective, forward-thinking, and ready to meet emerging challenges while staying true to the organization's faith-centered mission.

"For this reason I remind you to fan into flame the gift of God, which is in you... For the Spirit God gave us does not make us timid, but gives us power, love and self-discipline."

~2 Timothy 1:6–7

Leadership Impact

Secure leaders create a positive and empowering environment where team members feel valued, motivated, and equipped to achieve excellence. By prioritizing trust, collaboration, growth, support, and shared purpose, these leaders cultivate unity and resilience within their teams. Such an environment fosters both professional success and personal fulfillment, allowing individuals to thrive in their roles while contributing to the greater mission of service and protection.

This leadership approach not only strengthens team performance but also nurtures spiritual and emotional well-being, ensuring that every action reflects integrity, compassion, and faith. Secure leadership is more than direction—it is servant-hearted influence, guiding others through example, encouragement, and unwavering commitment to God's principles.

"Whoever wants to become great among you must be your servant, and whoever wants to be first must be your slave – just as the Son of

Man did not come to be served, but to serve, and to give his life as a ransom for many."

~ Matthew 20:26–28

Approach with Calm and Respect

Maintain Composure:

• Always remain calm, observant, and composed when approaching an individual who appears suspicious or is behaving unusually. Your demeanor sets the tone for the interaction. Avoid any actions or language that could escalate the situation, such as sudden movements, raised voices, or accusatory statements.

• Demonstrating self-control communicates confidence and authority, helping to diffuse tension and reduce the likelihood of confrontation. Remember, your goal is to de-escalate, not intimidate.

Speak Firmly and Respectfully:

• Address the individual using a calm yet confident tone, maintaining professionalism and courtesy. Speak clearly, avoid assumptions, and choose language that upholds the person's dignity and humanity.

• When possible, begin with neutral or open-ended questions (e.g., "Can I help you find someone?" or "Are you looking for a specific event?"). This approach allows you to assess intent while showing kindness and respect.

• Treat every person as a potential guest first and a threat second—unless clear danger is present. Compassionate awareness is key to maintaining both safety and ministry integrity.

"Everyone should be quick to listen, slow to speak and slow to become angry, because human anger does not produce the righteousness that God desires."

~ James 1:19–20

Initial Actions

Request Distance:

• Politely and calmly ask the individual to step aside from crowded or sensitive areas such as entrances, sanctuaries, or fellowship spaces. This helps to reduce potential risk while maintaining control of the situation in a respectful manner.

• Use courteous and non-threatening language—such as *"Would you mind stepping over here so we can talk privately?"*—to avoid embarrassment and preserve the individual's dignity.

• Maintain appropriate personal space and safe positioning, ensuring clear visibility of exits and the ability to summon assistance if necessary.

Assess Response:

• Carefully observe the person's behavior, body language, and tone of voice in response to your request. Cooperative, calm behavior may indicate a misunderstanding or a harmless situation, while refusal, agitation, or evasiveness should be treated as potential warning signs.

• If the individual becomes defensive or hostile or refuses to comply, do not escalate—instead, signal for support from other team members or law enforcement as appropriate. Trust your training and instincts; prioritize safety and de-escalation at all times.

"The prudent see danger and take refuge, but the simple keep going and pay the penalty."

~ Proverbs 22:3

Escalation Protocols

Engage Law Enforcement:

- If you observe weapons, threatening behavior, or receive credible threats directed toward the church or its members, contact law enforcement immediately. Provide clear and accurate details regarding the situation, including descriptions of individuals, observed actions, and any potential risks to others.
- Request the presence of an on-site law enforcement officer or appropriate emergency personnel to manage the incident. Allow police or other trained responders to take the lead upon arrival and fully cooperate with their instructions to ensure a lawful and professional resolution.

Prioritize Safety:

- The safety and protection of the congregation, staff, and volunteers must always come first. Avoid confronting or restraining individuals who may pose a danger. Instead, move people away from the immediate area and maintain communication with team members to coordinate response efforts.
- Whenever possible, rely on trained professionals—such as law enforcement or emergency response personnel—to handle potentially violent or high-risk situations.

Remember, your goal is to preserve life and restore peace, not to engage in physical confrontation.

"God is our refuge and strength, an ever-present help in trouble."

~ *Psalm 46:1*

Additional Tips

- **Stay Observant:**

Maintain continuous situational awareness during services and events. Stay alert for behavioral changes, unusual movements, or patterns that could indicate escalating tension or potential threats. Early recognition allows timely intervention and helps prevent incidents before they occur.

- **Communication Protocol:**

Establish and routinely review clear communication procedures within the church security team. Use designated channels (e.g., radios, code words, or signals) to relay information discreetly without alarming the congregation. Regular drills and briefings ensure that every team member understands their role and can respond swiftly and effectively when suspicious activity arises.

- **Document and Report:**

Thoroughly document all incidents or interactions involving suspicious individuals, noting key details such as time, location, descriptions, and actions taken. Submit reports to church leadership and local law enforcement as appropriate. Proper documentation supports accountability, follow-up investigations, and continuous improvement of security procedures.

"The horse is made ready for the day of battle, but victory rests with the Lord."

~ Proverbs 21:31

- **De-escalation and Resolution**
- Seek Professional Assistance:

When a situation escalates or becomes potentially dangerous, defer immediately to law enforcement or trained security professionals. Allow them to handle the matter safely and effectively, following established protocols. Remember that the priority is always the safety of everyone present—not confrontation or control.

- Follow Up:

After any incident, conduct a debriefing session with all involved personnel to review the response, assess what worked well, and identify areas for improvement. This ongoing evaluation strengthens the church's security procedures and ensures that lessons learned lead to better preparedness in the future.

By addressing suspicious situations with professionalism, calmness, and respect, while prioritizing safety and timely action, church security personnel help maintain peace and order within the worship environment.

Practices of Secure Leadership

Listening and Empathizing:

- Take time to genuinely listen to team members' perspectives, questions, and concerns. Understanding their experiences builds trust and promotes stronger relationships.

- **Providing Guidance, Not Dictates:**

  Offer direction, wisdom, and support without imposing solutions. Empower team members to think critically and make sound decisions within established frameworks.

- **Building Trust Through Consistency:**

Demonstrate integrity and reliability in all leadership actions. Consistency fosters confidence and respect among those you lead.

- **Celebrating Team Achievements:**

Publicly recognize and celebrate accomplishments. Gratitude strengthens morale, reinforces unity, and reminds the team that their efforts are valued.

- **Encouraging Ownership and Accountability:**

Promote a sense of shared mission by encouraging each member to take ownership of their responsibilities. Accountability builds both confidence and discipline.

- **Leading by Example:**

Model the behavior, professionalism, and values you expect from your team. Leadership credibility grows through actions, not only words.

- **Continuous Development and Feedback:**

Encourage a mindset of lifelong learning and regular reflection. Offer constructive feedback and recognize progress to help individuals grow in skill and character.

- **Adaptability and Flexibility:**

Remain open to feedback and willing to adjust strategies as situations or environments change. Flexibility demonstrates wisdom and humility in leadership.

Secure leadership is founded on trust, empowerment, and consistency. Leaders who embody these principles create an environment where team members feel valued, motivated, and confident to perform at their best—fulfilling the mission of protection and service in unity and faith.

"But the wisdom that comes from heaven is first of all pure; then peace-loving, considerate, submissive, full of mercy and good fruit, impartial and sincere."

~ James 3:17

Confronting a Suspicious Person

In a church or faith-based setting, addressing suspicious behavior requires careful communication, discernment, and calm professionalism. The goal is to preserve safety while maintaining compassion and respect for individuals.

Communication Approach

1. **Maintain Calmness and Respect:**

• Speak quietly but firmly. A calm tone conveys confidence and reduces tension.

• Show respect for the person's dignity; avoid judgmental language or actions that could escalate the situation.

2. **Use Clear and Direct Language:**

• Clearly communicate your concerns or requests in plain, respectful terms.

• Avoid confrontational or accusatory phrasing; focus on safety and understanding.

3. **Request Compliance:**

• Politely ask the individual to move away from the main congregation or gathering area for a private conversation.

• Maintain a safe physical distance and clear access to exits.

Actions to Take

Assess the Response:

Observe how the person reacts. Refusal to comply, hostility, or agitation may signal a higher threat level and require immediate assistance.

Engage Law Enforcement:

• If you see weapons, hear specific threats, or detect clear signs of danger, contact law enforcement immediately.

• Request an on-site officer or call emergency services. Once police arrive, defer authority to them and cooperate fully.

Ensure Safety of Others:

• Prioritize the safety of the congregation and staff.

• If necessary, discreetly move people to a safe location or initiate partial evacuation under the guidance of law enforcement or leadership.

Document Details:

• Record all relevant details—descriptions, statements, and actions observed.

• Share this documentation with law enforcement and church leadership for follow-up and review.

"A gentle answer turns away wrath, but a harsh word stirs up anger."

~ Proverbs 15:1

Additional Considerations

1. Avoid Confrontation Alone:

Whenever possible, do not approach a suspicious individual alone. Always ensure that another trusted security team member, usher, or staff person accompanies you to provide both safety and witness support.

2. Follow Security Protocols:

Adhere strictly to your church's established security guidelines and emergency procedures. Consistency ensures predictable responses and minimizes confusion during critical moments.

3. Provide Support:

Following any incident, offer comfort and reassurance to congregation members, staff, or volunteers who may feel anxious or unsettled. Emotional care after an event is as important as the physical response, reinforcing trust and stability within the church community.

4. Review and Learn:

After each situation is resolved, conduct a post-incident debriefing. Evaluate what occurred, identify strengths, and discuss areas for improvement. Continuous learning fosters growth and ensures that the church's security approach remains effective, responsive, and compassionate.

Confronting suspicious behavior or potential threats in a church setting requires balance—firmness without aggression, vigilance with compassion, and readiness guided by faith. Prioritize the safety of every individual involved and always rely on law enforcement and trained professionals when serious threats emerge.

"Listen to advice and accept discipline, and at the end you will be counted among the wise."

~ Proverbs 19:20

Understanding Church Roles and Responsibilities

The effectiveness of church security and safety relies on clear coordination among all ministries and personnel. Each group contributes uniquely to maintaining a secure, welcoming, and spiritually nurturing environment. Below is a breakdown of typical roles and how they align with safety and emergency preparedness:

Every role within a faith-based organization contributes uniquely to the safety, order, and spiritual well-being of the congregation. By defining duties clearly and fostering cooperation, churches can maintain both a welcoming and secure environment.

Church Leaders

- Provide Guidance and Direction:
- Offer spiritual leadership, vision, and oversight for the congregation. Lead decision-making regarding church operations, activities, and safety policies.
- Building Evacuation:
- Develop, communicate, and rehearse evacuation procedures for emergencies. During drills or real events, ensure that congregants are safely guided out of the facility in an orderly manner.

Security Team

- Leadership Focus:
- Oversee all security operations and protocols within the church, coordinating safety procedures for both internal and external areas.
- Internal and External Perimeter:
- Monitor entrances, parking lots, and surrounding grounds. Enforce access controls and deter unauthorized entry to maintain a safe environment for worship and fellowship.

Congregation

- Feeling and Being Safe:
- Every member plays a part in church security. Congregants should follow safety guidelines, remain observant, and report concerns promptly. A culture of shared responsibility strengthens protection for all.

Greeter

- Front-Line Defense:
- Welcome guests warmly while maintaining awareness and observation. Greeters serve as the first point of contact, identifying suspicious behavior or unusual items before they enter.

Usher

- Second-Line Defense:
- Support congregation order by assisting with seating, responding discreetly to disruptions, and notifying security or leadership of potential issues within the worship area.

Medical Team

- Emergency Response:

- Provide immediate medical care in cases of injury or illness. Maintain first-aid kits, emergency supplies, and readiness during all services and events.

Additional Considerations

- Collaboration and Training:
- Strengthen communication and cooperation among all ministries through joint training, drills, and coordination meetings.
- Awareness and Vigilance:
- Encourage all members to remain observant and to report suspicious behavior or safety concerns promptly.
- Continuous Improvement:
- Conduct regular reviews of security procedures, incorporating feedback and updating protocols to address new risks or lessons learned.

Summary:

Each ministry and role is essential to maintaining a secure, compassionate, and welcoming atmosphere. Through clear responsibilities, teamwork, and faith-driven cooperation, the church can thrive as both a spiritual sanctuary and a safe haven.

Safety Response Team Members

Safety Response Team (SRT) - Roles and Responsibilities

The Safety Response Team serves as the core unit responsible for coordinating emergency preparedness, communication, and immediate response actions during critical incidents. A well-trained SRT ensures that every emergency—whether medical, environmental, or security-related—is handled swiftly, safely, and in accordance with established procedures.

"Be shepherds of God's flock that is under your care… watching over them willingly, as God wants you to."

~ 1 Peter 5:2

General Member Responsibilities

All SRT members are expected to:

- Be thoroughly familiar with the Emergency Operations Plan (EOP) and notification process.
- Know the locations of all key emergency resources (fire alarms, extinguishers, exits, first aid kits, and AEDs).

- Respond promptly to all alarms and instructions from team leaders.
- Assist with evacuation or shelter-in-place procedures as required.
- Aid individuals with mobility limitations or disabilities.
- Help identify missing, injured, or trapped individuals and report them immediately to the Incident Coordinator.

Building Coordinator

Responsible for overall facility awareness and liaison with emergency agencies.

- Maintain up-to-date floor plans and evacuation procedures for all major scenarios (fire, tornado, and medical emergency).
- Receive and consolidate status reports from Incident Coordinator(s).
- Relay updates to fire, police, and EMS personnel on scene.
- Coordinate evacuations and other emergency actions with public safety agencies.
- Assist with long-term emergency planning, team recruitment, and training coordination.

Incident Coordinator

Acts as the on-scene leader during emergencies until relieved by senior leadership or official responders.

- Implement the Emergency Operations Plan (EOP) and direct response efforts.
- Assign tasks to SRT members based on the situation.
- Maintain communication with all response personnel and ensure 911 has been called.
- Evaluate the situation and provide clear, concise instructions to staff and volunteers.
- Ensure proper reporting and documentation of the incident.

Medical Response Team

Provides first aid and coordinates medical care until professional responders arrive.

- Administer CPR, AED, and first aid within training limits.
- Conduct primary medical assessments and communicate patient status to EMS personnel upon arrival.

- Maintain medical supplies and equipment in accessible, working condition.
- Document all medical responses for post-incident review.

Safety Response Team Members (Floor/Area Leads)

Serve as operational hands-on personnel for specific zones or buildings.

- Conduct floor sweeps during evacuations and report cleared sections to the Incident Coordinator.
- Implement lockdown or shelter-in-place procedures when instructed.
- Coordinate with maintenance/trustees to eliminate hazards and restore safety conditions.
- Maintain communication devices (radios and cell phones) for situational awareness.
- Wear high-visibility identification (vests or badges) during emergencies.

Leader Quick-Action Responsibilities

Medical Emergency:

- Call 911 immediately and provide the detailed location and nature of the emergency.

- Administer first aid within the scope of training until professionals arrive.

- **Fire or Smoke Emergency:**
  - Activate the manual fire alarm and begin evacuation.
  - Call 911 from a safe location and report situation details.
  - Attempt to extinguish small fires only if safe to do so.

- **Building Evacuation:**
  - Guide members and visitors along designated routes.
  - Assist individuals with disabilities.
  - Do not re-enter until cleared by emergency responders or the Incident Coordinator.
- **Tornado/Severe Weather:**
  - Move all occupants to designated shelter areas (interior hallways, basements).
  - Monitor weather alerts continuously.
  - Remain sheltered until authorities give the all-clear.

- **Intruder/Active Shooter:**
  - Lock or barricade doors and turn off lights.
  - Call 911 discreetly; stay quiet and hidden.
  - Follow **Run–Hide–Fight** or as circumstances allow.

Ongoing Preparedness and Maintenance

- Conduct regular training and drills to reinforce readiness and build confidence.
- Maintain an up-to-date emergency contact list and distribute copies to leaders and volunteers.
- Provide clear communication channels (radios, intercoms, group text alerts).
- Collaborate closely with local emergency responders to align plans with official community procedures.
- Review and update all safety procedures annually or after any major incident.

"Plans fail for lack of counsel, but with many advisers they succeed."

~ Proverbs 15:22

Warning Signs & General Safety Information

Recognizing early warning signs and responding quickly can prevent harm. Use the guidance below to educate staff, volunteers, and congregants and to standardize reporting and escalation.

Concerning Behaviors (Report Immediately)

- Threatens harm or talks about killing others (report immediately to law enforcement).

- Frequently starts or participates in fights or aggressive behavior.
- Loses temper easily; poor impulse control with unpredictable behavior.
- Persistent vulgar/menacing language with escalating hostility.
- Graphic drawings/writings depicting death or violence.
- Repeated involvement in domestic violence incidents.
- Frustration that escalates into uncontrollable physical violence.
- Action: Document specifics, notify leadership, and contact law enforcement per policy. Prioritize safety and confidentiality.

Hazard Awareness Briefs (Localize and Rotate)

- Flooding—Avoid floodways; move to higher ground; never drive through water.
- Hazardous Materials—Evacuate upwind if instructed; avoid contact; report precise location.
- Severe Weather—Know shelter areas, heed alerts, and conduct shelter drills.

- Earthquakes—Drop-Cover-Hold On during shaking, evacuate when safe.
- Fire—Know routes; locate extinguishers; report fires; use PASS (Pull, Aim, Squeeze, Sweep).

Program Tips

- Conduct regular safety training and drills for staff, volunteers, and congregants.
- Establish clear channels to report concerns (hotline, QR form, designated leaders).
- Collaborate with local authorities and emergency services on plan alignment and training.
- Encourage open dialogue and non-retaliatory reporting of suspicious behaviors.

Recognizing Warning Signs of Potential Threats

Understanding behavioral indicators that could signal potential violence is critical for prevention. While no single sign guarantees harmful intent, awareness and timely response can help mitigate risks.

1. History of Violence:
2. Escalating or repeated aggressive behavior, especially if unresolved or ignored.

2. Verbal Threats:

3. Direct or indirect expressions of harm—spoken, written, or online—should always be taken seriously.

3. Intense Anger or Hostility:

4. Persistent or disproportionate anger that may manifest as confrontation or resentment.

4. Social Isolation:

5. Withdrawal from social interaction, accompanied by feelings of rejection or grievance.

5. Obsession with Weapons:

6. Fixation on firearms or violence, shown through speech, social media, or behavior.

6. Mental Health Concerns:

7. Untreated or worsening mental health conditions, especially those involving paranoia or delusions.

7. Substance Abuse:

8. Alcohol or drug dependency that impairs judgment and heightens aggression.

8. Lack of Empathy:

9. A consistent inability to show compassion or regard for others' well-being.

9. Intimidation or Bullying:

10. A pattern of harassment, manipulation, or threats toward others.

10. Sudden Behavioral Changes:

11. Noticeable mood swings, expressions of hopelessness, or erratic behavior.

Note:

These indicators are not definitive predictors of violence. However, patterns or combinations of these behaviors warrant careful observation, documentation, and consultation with mental health professionals or law enforcement as appropriate.

"Carry each other's burdens, and in this way you will fulfill the law of Christ."

~ Galatians 6:2

Congregational Actions in an Active Shooter Situation

Encountering an active shooter is a life-threatening situation that requires immediate and decisive action.

Being mentally prepared and familiar with response options can greatly increase your chances of survival.

1. Be Aware of Your Surroundings

7. Stay alert at all times—know where exits, hiding places, and barriers are located.

8. Trust your instincts. If something feels off, take it seriously and act quickly.

2. Have an Escape Plan

9. Identify primary and secondary escape routes wherever you go—churches, workplaces, schools, or public events.

10. Rehearse how you would exit quickly under stress.

3. Run, Hide, Fight

This framework is recognized by law enforcement as the most effective survival model:

• **Run:**

- If it's safe to escape, run immediately and encourage others to follow.
- Leave belongings behind—your life is the priority.
- Keep your hands visible to police and obey their instructions once outside.

• **Hide:**

- If escape isn't possible, find a secure hiding place.

- Lock or barricade doors, silence your phone, and remain out of view.
- Stay low, quiet, and calm until authorities arrive.

- **Fight:**
- As a last resort, if your life is in immediate danger, fight back with determination.
- Use improvised weapons (chairs, fire extinguishers, and tools) to incapacitate the shooter.
- Commit fully—your goal is to disrupt or stop the threat to save lives.

4. Call for Help

11. When safe, call 911 or local emergency services.
12. Give your name, location, description of the shooter, number of weapons, and any injuries observed.

5. Communicate with Others

13. Use text or social media to inform trusted contacts of your status and location.

14. Keep messages brief to avoid detection and network overload.

6. Follow Law Enforcement Instructions

15. Stay calm when police arrive.

16. Keep your hands raised and fingers spread.

17. Avoid sudden movements or shouting—officers' priority is to identify threats quickly.

7. Prepare Mentally

- Visualize your actions before a crisis occurs.
- Discuss scenarios with your team or congregation security group to build confidence and readiness.

Additional Tips

- **Stay Low and Move Quickly:** Minimize your visibility and exposure when moving.
- **Do Not Play Dead:** Remain alert; shooters may continue targeting anyone they perceive as a threat.

- **Stay Informed:** Follow verified updates from law enforcement or emergency management.

"Have I not commanded you? Be strong and courageous. Do not be afraid; do not be discouraged, for the Lord your God will be with you wherever you go."

~ Joshua 1:9

Summary

Lockdown and active-shooter procedures are designed to protect lives through calm, disciplined action.

Preparation, awareness, and cooperation with authorities are essential.

When coupled with faith and prayer, these practical measures enable the church to fulfill its calling to be a safe haven—a place where God's people can worship, serve, and find peace even amid uncertainty.

Leadership Oversight and Response Coordination During and After a Critical Incident

"Where there is no guidance, a people falls, but in an abundance of counselors there is safety."

~ Proverbs 11:14

In times of crisis, effective leadership becomes both a spiritual and practical anchor for the congregation. Leaders must act decisively, communicate clearly, and reflect Christ's peace amid chaos. *"For God is not the author of confusion, but of peace"* (1 Corinthians 14:33). The following guidelines help ensure safety, order, and compassion during emergencies.

Incident Control Focal Point:

- Establish a clear chain of command before an incident occurs. Identify who assumes control if the primary leader or security director is incapacitated.
- Use plain language and radio or phone communication to coordinate law enforcement, security, and staff.
- Ensure everyone understands their role—security, ushers, medical, and leadership—so response actions are coordinated and not duplicated.

Coordinate with Law Enforcement:

- Work alongside responding officers and emergency personnel. Provide them with immediate access to floor plans, keys, and relevant site information.

- Maintain Calm and Faith: Lead by example—speak with composure and reassurance. A calm leader encourages a calm response.

Maintain Accountability Protocols:

- Once safe, conduct accountability checks to verify the safety of staff, volunteers, and congregants.
- Designate team members to record names and locations of individuals who are accounted for or missing.
- Provide this information to law enforcement and emergency responders as soon as practicable.
- Support Family Reunification: Designate team members to help families reconnect safely and discreetly.

Media and Communications:

- **Designate Media Liaisons**: Appoint a single spokesperson (often a senior leader or communications director).
- Provide factual, verified information only—avoid speculation or details that could compromise ongoing investigations.
- Prepare a pre-approved statement template to use immediately following an incident.

- Guard Privacy and Integrity: Respect the dignity and privacy of victims and families. Avoid speculation or blame.

Assembly Area and Crowd Control:

- Identify safe assembly points away from the immediate danger zone but still accessible to first responders.
- Train ushers or security volunteers to help direct individuals calmly toward these areas.
- Keep exits clear and provide assistance to those with mobility challenges.
- Support Vulnerable Individuals: Provide extra assistance to children, the elderly, and individuals with disabilities.

Medical Support and Post-Incident Care:

- **Activate Medical Response:** Ensure basic first-aid supplies and trained personnel are available at every major event or service.
- Coordinate with emergency medical services to treat injured individuals and document care rendered.
- After the event, arrange emotional and spiritual support for those affected, including counseling or debrief sessions.

Recovery and After-Action Review:

- After the incident, conduct a formal debrief with leadership, security, and local authorities.
- Identify lessons learned, update procedures, and reinforce training based on real-world outcomes.
- Communicate openly with the congregation about recovery steps, emphasizing resilience and unity.
- Reinforce Faith and Resilience: Encourage healing through worship, prayer gatherings, and fellowship.
- Update Plans and Training: Revise security protocols and retrain staff based on lessons learned.

"Let all things be done decently and in order."

~1 Corinthians 14:40

Post-Incident Debriefing and Continuous Improvement

- **Conduct Structured Debriefings:**
- After an incident, gather key leaders, responders, and witnesses to review the sequence of events.
- Identify what worked well, what challenges arose, and what can be improved for future response efforts.

- **Document Lessons Learned:**

- Maintain written records of lessons learned and update your Emergency Operations Plan accordingly.
- Use these insights to refine protocols, reinforce training, and strengthen the ministry's overall resilience.

- **Provide Care and Restoration:**
- Recognize the emotional and spiritual impact of critical incidents. Offer counseling, prayer, and pastoral support to all who were affected—including staff and volunteers.
- Encourage a return to normalcy through faith-based healing and community unity.

"He gives strength to the weary and increases the power of the weak."

~ *Isaiah 40:29*

Effective leadership during and after a critical incident requires proactive planning, clear communication, and spiritual discernment. By establishing defined roles, fostering preparedness, and maintaining faith amid uncertainty, leadership teams can coordinate incident control, accountability, media response, assembly-area management, and medical support with excellence and compassion.

Section 4: Emergency Response Plan

Introduction

Developing an effective Emergency Response Plan (ERP) begins with understanding the potential risks your church or ministry may face. Conducting a risk assessment is the first essential step—identifying possible emergency scenarios allows leadership to determine what resources are needed and to establish the appropriate plans, policies, and procedures.

An emergency plan should align with the church's mission, ministry goals, and safety performance objectives. Above all, every church—regardless of size—should develop and implement a plan that protects members, visitors, volunteers, and staff. This portion of planning is often referred to as "Protective Actions for Life Safety."

"The wise store up knowledge, but the mouth of a fool invites ruin."

~ Proverbs 10:14

Incident Stabilization and Response Actions

Once immediate danger has passed, church leaders and trained responders should take actions to stabilize the situation and minimize damage. Examples include:

• **Providing First Aid and CPR:** Trained team members can save lives before emergency responders arrive.

• **Using Fire Extinguishers:** Properly trained individuals can extinguish small fires before they spread.

• **Containing Minor Chemical Spills:** Trained staff can help prevent environmental damage and protect property.

• **Managing Utilities:** Turning off gas, electricity, or water as directed to prevent further hazards.

Certain emergencies—such as severe weather—can often be forecast hours in advance, giving the church valuable time to prepare and protect people and property.

"A prudent person foresees danger and takes precautions."

— *Proverbs 22:3*

Post-Incident Actions

After an emergency, the response does not end. The plan should include clear procedures for:

1. **Damage Assessment** - Inspecting and documenting the extent of structural or property damage.
2. **Salvage Operations** - Recovering and securing usable property, equipment, and records.
3. **Protection of Undamaged Property** - Taking steps to safeguard areas not directly affected.
4. **Cleanup and Restoration** - Removing debris, ensuring safety, and preparing the facility for reoccupation.

These steps help minimize further disruption and promote a quicker recovery for the ministry.

Developing and Implementing a Comprehensive Emergency Plan

Creating an Emergency Response Plan (ERP) for a church or ministry involves more than compliance—it is an act of stewardship, care, and responsibility for God's people.

"Be shepherds of God's flock that is under your care... not because you must, but because you are willing."

~1 Peter 5:2

A well-prepared Emergency Response Plan for a church or religious facility should:

• Identify potential hazards and corresponding response procedures.

• Define roles and responsibilities for leadership, staff, and volunteers.

• Include communication protocols for both internal teams and external responders.

• Establish training schedules, evacuation maps, and emergency contact lists.

• Outline recovery and restoration strategies following an incident.

"Let all things be done decently and in order."

~ 1 Corinthians 14:40

The following steps outline the essential components of a comprehensive emergency response plan that prioritizes life safety, minimizes risk, and strengthens resilience.

1. Conduct a Risk Assessment

• **Identify Potential Emergency Scenarios:**

Evaluate all potential hazards and threats that may affect the church facility and surrounding area, such as fire, severe weather, acts of violence, medical emergencies, and chemical releases.

- **Consider Local Context and History:**

Review historical data, regional risks, and local regulations. Coordinate with community emergency management agencies to understand likely scenarios and required preparedness actions.

"The prudent see danger and take refuge, but the simple keep going and pay the penalty."

~Proverbs 27:12

2. Define Protective Actions for Life Safety

Protective actions are the cornerstone of every emergency response plan. They ensure the safety of members, visitors, and staff during various emergencies.

- **Building Evacuation (Fire Drills):**

Establish clear evacuation procedures and conduct routine fire drills. Mark exits, assign evacuation coordinators, and ensure routes remain unobstructed at all times.

- **Sheltering from Severe Weather:**

Designate safe shelter locations within the facility—such as interior rooms, basements, or hallways—away from windows and exterior walls. Practice moving to these areas during drills.

- **Shelter-in-Place for Airborne Hazards:**

Develop a shelter-in-place plan for chemical or hazardous-material incidents. Identify rooms that can be sealed off and stock them with emergency supplies.

- **Lockdown Procedures:**

Create and practice lockdown protocols to secure the facility during an act of violence or an active threat. Include clear communication signals and steps for barricading or hiding safely.

"Let all things be done decently and in order." ~ 1 Corinthians 14:40

3. Establish Priorities During Emergencies

- **Life Safety:**

Always prioritize the protection of life above all else. Ensure all personnel and volunteers understand that every action taken should serve to preserve life.

- **Incident Stabilization:**

After ensuring safety, focus on controlling the situation to prevent further harm or damage. Coordinate with emergency responders to support their efforts.

4. Implement Stabilization Measures

• First Aid and CPR:

Train designated personnel in basic first aid and CPR. Ensure kits are easily accessible throughout the facility.

• Fire Extinguisher Use:

Provide fire extinguisher training for staff to handle small fires safely while awaiting fire services.

• Chemical Spill Containment:

Create simple containment protocols for minor spills, ensuring staff know how to act safely without exposure.

• Building Utilities and Systems:

Appoint trained individuals to manage critical systems (electricity, water, HVAC) to prevent further hazards during emergencies.

"He heals the brokenhearted and binds up their wounds."

~ Psalm 147:3

5. Prepare for Forecasted Severe Weather Events

• Establish Preparedness Protocols:

Monitor weather alerts and activate preparedness procedures early. Designate staff to communicate updates and coordinate sheltering.

• Resource Allocation:

Maintain emergency supply kits, flashlights, radios, blankets, and communication tools. Assign team members to retrieve and distribute supplies as needed.

"He makes the storm a calm, so that the waves thereof are still."

~ *Psalm 107:29*

6. Plan for Post-Incident Actions

• Damage Assessment:

After an incident, document all structural and property damage. Take photos, record descriptions, and communicate findings to insurance and restoration teams.

• Salvage and Protection:

Recover undamaged property, secure important documents, and take measures to prevent additional loss.

• Cleanup and Restoration:

Develop safe cleanup procedures. Coordinate with professional services if needed, and ensure the facility is safe before resuming normal operations.

Additional Considerations

• Training and Drills:

Conduct regular training sessions and emergency drills for staff, volunteers, and congregants. Reinforce procedures until they become second nature.

• Communication and Notification:

Establish clear communication protocols to notify occupants, staff, and emergency responders quickly. Consider mass text alerts or loudspeaker systems.

• Documentation and Review:

Maintain written records of your emergency response plan, drills, and revisions. Review and update the plan annually or after major incidents.

• Community Collaboration:

Work closely with local emergency management agencies, fire departments, and law enforcement. Building these relationships enhances coordination and response capabilities.

"Plans fail for lack of counsel, but with many advisers they succeed."

— Proverbs 15:22

Conclusion

By following these structured steps and incorporating protective actions for life safety, churches can enhance preparedness, mitigate risk, and protect every individual entrusted to their care. A well-developed Emergency Response Plan is both a practical safeguard and a spiritual commitment—demonstrating wisdom, compassion, and faithful stewardship in protecting God's people.

Protective Actions for Life Safety in Multi-Building Facilities

Establishing clear, well-practiced protective actions across all church buildings ensures safety, reduces confusion, and allows leaders to care for their congregation effectively during any crisis. Whether your ministry operates in one facility or several, consistency and communication are key.

"Let all things be done decently and in order."

~ 1 Corinthians 14:40

1. Evacuation

- **Develop Evacuation Procedures:**
- Identify primary and secondary evacuation routes for each building within the church property.
- Designate assembly areas outside each structure where evacuees can gather for accountability.
- Assign specific team members to guide individuals—particularly the elderly, children, or those with mobility limitations—to safety.

- • **Conduct Regular Evacuation Drills:**
- Schedule routine fire and evacuation drills to ensure all occupants are familiar with exit routes and procedures.
- Document each drill and evaluate performance to identify improvements and strengthen readiness.

"The wise store up knowledge."

~ Proverbs 10:14

2. Sheltering

- • **Identify Safe Shelter Areas:**
- Designate **safe shelter locations** within each building (e.g., basements, interior hallways) for protection during severe weather such as tornadoes or hurricanes.
- Ensure shelters are **structurally sound** and away from windows, exterior doors, or glass.
- • **Communicate Sheltering Procedures:**
- Clearly post sheltering instructions and direct staff on how to guide congregants calmly to designated areas.
- Conduct occasional walkthroughs to help everyone become familiar with these locations.

"He is my refuge and my fortress, my God, in whom I trust."

~ ***Psalm 91:2***

3. Shelter-In-Place

- • **Establish Shelter-In-Place Protocols:**
- Prepare guidelines for sheltering in place during external hazards, such as chemical spills or airborne contaminants.

- Train staff to seal doors, vents, and windows when appropriate and to minimize exposure to outdoor air.
- • **Train Occupants on Shelter-In-Place Procedures:**
- Conduct informational sessions and practical demonstrations so that staff and volunteers know the correct steps to take when sheltering indoors.

"You will keep in perfect peace those whose minds are steadfast, because they trust in you." ~ Isaiah 26:3

4. Lockdown

- • **Implement Lockdown Procedures:**
- Define the specific conditions that warrant a lockdown, such as acts of violence or credible security threats.
- Establish clear protocols for **run, hide, or fight** actions, depending on proximity to the threat.
- **Designate lockdown assembly zones** that offer protection and concealment until authorities issue an all-clear.

- • **Conduct Lockdown Drills:**
- Practice lockdown procedures regularly with staff, teachers, and ministry leaders.

- Review and debrief after each drill to reinforce preparedness and confidence.

"Be strong and courageous; do not be afraid or discouraged, for the Lord your God is with you." ~ Joshua 1:9

5. Earthquake Preparedness

- • **Develop Earthquake Response Plans:**
- Identify safe areas (under sturdy furniture, against interior walls) where occupants can drop, cover, and hold on during shaking.
- Plan for post-earthquake evacuation once it is safe while ensuring structures are stable.

- • Provide Earthquake Safety Training:
- Teach occupants and volunteers the basic Drop, Cover, and Hold On technique and discuss safety actions for both during and after an earthquake.

6. Coordination with Building Managers

- **Collaborate on Multi-Building Planning:**
- Coordinate with facility managers, tenants, or neighboring property owners to ensure consistency across the entire campus.
- Share emergency plans, maps, and resources so all facilities respond cohesively.

7. Additional Considerations

- **Communication and Notification Systems:**
- Install or integrate mass notification systems, intercoms, and mobile alerts to communicate real-time updates during emergencies.

- **Resource Allocation and Preparedness:**
- Keep essential emergency resources available—first-aid kits, flashlights, radios, and other supplies in each building.

- **Regular Review and Updates:**

- Review your emergency plan annually or following major incidents or facility changes. Update contact lists, maps, and procedures as needed.

"Plans fail for lack of counsel, but with many advisers they succeed." ~ Proverbs 15:22

Summary

- By incorporating these protective actions for life safety into your emergency response plan—and by practicing them regularly, your church or ministry will be better equipped to respond quickly, effectively, and faithfully to any emergency. Collaboration among leadership, staff, volunteers, and community partners ensures unified action and a resilient ministry that safeguards every soul entrusted to its care.

"God is our refuge and strength, an ever-present help in trouble." ~ Psalm 46:1

Section 5: Displaying Emergency Telephone Numbers

- In every emergency, speed of communication can save lives. Ensuring that emergency telephone numbers are clearly posted and accessible throughout the facility helps staff, volunteers, and visitors respond quickly and confidently.

1. Visible Locations

- Post emergency contact signage in high-traffic and strategic areas, including:

- Entrances and exits

- Hallways and lobbies

- Classrooms, offices, and meeting spaces

- Restrooms, break areas, and fellowship halls

- Use large, legible fonts and ensure signage remains visible even during power outages (consider glow-in-the-dark materials).

2. Digital Displays

- Use digital bulletin boards or monitors to cycle through emergency numbers and safety reminders.
- Include emergency contact information in church newsletters, bulletins, or electronic announcements for quick reference by the congregation.

3. Near Communication Devices

- Place emergency contact lists next to telephones, intercom systems, and two-way radios.
- Ensure all staff know the location of these devices and how to operate them.

4. Include Relevant Emergency Numbers

- **911:**

Clearly display the universal emergency number *911* for immediate police, fire, or medical response.

- **Local Emergency Numbers:**
- If your area does not use 9-1-1 service, list the direct numbers for fire, police, and EMS dispatch.

- **Additional Key Contacts:**
- Include local and organizational numbers such as
- - Fire Department
- - Police Department

- - Emergency Medical Services (EMS)
- - Poison Control Center
- - Facility or Security Director
- - Maintenance/Building Management

"Do not withhold good from those to whom it is due, when it is in your power to act." ~ Proverbs 3:27

Conclusion

- Clear communication and visible emergency contact information empower staff and congregants to act swiftly and decisively. Posting and maintaining these resources throughout the facility ensures that when moments matter most, help can be reached without hesitation.

Daytime/Nighttime Business Hours Contacts:

Daytime				
	Name	Contact Number (Daytime)	Contact Number (Nighttime)	24-Hour Emergency Phone Number
Building Maintenance / Trustees				
Pastor(s)/Minister(s)				
Building Coordinator(s)				
Medical Response Team Members				
Emergency Response Team Members				
Nighttime				
	Name	Contact Number (Daytime)	Contact Number (Nighttime)	24-Hour Emergency Phone Number
Building Maintenance / Trustees				

Pastor(s)/Minister(s)				
Building Coordinator(s)				
Medical Response Team Members				
Emergency Response Team Members				
	Local Police Department	Fire Department	Ambulance/Medical Services	
Other Emergency Contact(s)				

Additional Tips:

- Ensure all team members are aware of their roles and responsibilities during emergencies.
- Regularly update and distribute the contact list to relevant staff and volunteers.
- Include local emergency service contact numbers for immediate assistance during emergencies.
- Maintain a centralized and easily accessible location for the contact list within the facility.

Appendix A — Threat Call Checklist (Bomb/Violence/Custody)

Remain calm and keep the caller on the line if it is safe to do so. Use a prearranged signal to alert another person to listen/record. Capture as much detail as possible for law enforcement. Do not hang up unless instructed by authorities.

Exact Time of Call
Date
Exact Words of Caller

Caller Profile

Voice (Male/Female; Adult/Youth; Est. Age)
Tone (Calm/Nervous/Angry/Excited/Slurred/Loud/Whisper/Disguised/Accent/Crying/Giggling/Stressed/Nasal/Other)
If familiar, sounds like
Background Noises (Music/Children/Typing/Aircraft/Machinery/Traffic/Other)

Questions to Ask (Record Verbatim):

When is the device/event going to occur?

Where is it located?

What does it look like?

What kind is it?

Method of activation (mechanical/clock/motion/chemical)?

Method of deactivation?

Did you place it? Why?

Where are you calling from?

What is your address?

What is your name?

Call Received By
Department
Extension

Immediate Steps

Call 911: say, "We received a bomb/threat call," and provide location/extension.

Preserve notes and the phone line if possible; follow law enforcement instructions.

Stay calm and ensure building leadership is notified per policy. Taking detailed notes and promptly reporting the threat to emergency services is essential for ensuring the safety and security of everyone involved. Do not hang up the call until instructed to do so by authorities.

Emergency Telephone Numbers

Format and Design

- **Use clear, legible fonts:** Large sans-serif fonts: a minimum of 24–36 pt for headings and 16–20 pt for body. Readable from 10–15 feet.
- **High contrast:** Dark text on light background (or the reverse). Avoid busy images behind text.
- **Bilingual where needed:** Provide numbers in the primary languages of your congregation/community.

Regular Review and Updates

- **Periodic checks:** Inspect signs quarterly and after any number/role changes.
- **Training & awareness:** Brief staff/volunteers on where signs are posted and how to use the numbers.

Communication Channels

- **Announcements and reminders:** Include brief safety reminders during services or large events.
- **Educational materials:** Add numbers and "what to do" tips to bulletins, newcomer packets, and email newsletters.

Community Resources

- **Verify with local authorities:** Confirm correct non-emergency and after-hours lines.
- **Support public campaigns:** Share city/county preparedness messages.

"Let all things be done decently and in order." – *1 Cor. 14:40*

Evacuation Plan — Development and Implementation

1) Warning System and Preparation

- **Evaluate warning systems:** Test fire alarms, PA systems, and backup devices (air horns/whistles). Conduct sound-familiarization drills.

- **Ensure sufficient exits:** At least two remotely located exits from hazardous areas on every floor; illuminated EXIT signs; paths kept clear.

2) Evacuation Team Leadership

- **Appoint leaders:** Name an **Evacuation Team Leader** and **floor/room wardens** (Each occupied room has one).

- **Plan for assistance:** Maintain a confidential list of individuals needing mobility/other support; assign "buddies."

- **Coordinate with Fire Dept.:** Incorporate their guidance for persons with disabilities.

3) Accountability and Tracking

- **Member/visitor lists:** Keep updated rosters and a same-day visitor log at reception.

- **Assembly-area check-in:** Wardens bring lists to the rally point; report "all clear," missing, or injured to the Incident/Building Coordinator.

4) Alternate Exit Plans

- **Pre-plan alternates:** Train wardens to redirect when primaries are blocked (fire, debris, or spill).

Ongoing

- **Drills and refreshers:** Conduct at least 2x per year; debrief and update maps/procedures.

- **Clear comms:** Assign radio channels or code phrases; confirm who calls 911 and who meets responders.

"The prudent see danger and take refuge." – Prov. 27:12

Sheltering & Lockdown Procedures

A) Sheltering (Tornado/Severe Weather)

1. **Distinct warning signal** (sirens/intercom/text).
2. **Shelter locations:** Basements/interior rooms or hallways away from glass; verify capacity.
3. **Early warning:** NOAA weather radio; opt-in SMS/email alerts; monitor local media.

B) Shelter-in-Place (Chemical/Hazardous Release)

- **Plan & announce:** Move away from windows to interior rooms on **upper floors** (Avoid basements for heavy gases).

- **Immediate actions:** Bring people indoors; close/lock exterior doors/windows; **shut HVAC/air intakes**.
- **Remain sheltered** until officials give an all-clear; maintain info flow (radio/phone).

C) Lockdown (Act of Violence)

- **Immediate actions:** Lock/barricade, turn lights off, silence phones, and be out of sightlines.
- **Communications:** Multiple trained broadcasters to issue lockdown from safe locations (intercom, text).
- **Run–Hide–Fight:** Teach decision-making based on proximity to threat; practice regularly.

"Be strong and courageous… for the Lord your God is with you." – Josh. 1:9

Essential Contacts — Daytime & 24/7 (Template)

Instruction: Keep one laminated copy at each phone/radio point; one digital copy on shared drive; update at least quarterly.

Daytime/Business Hours

1. **Building Maintenance/Trustees:** [Name] – [Phone]
2. **Pastor/Minister(s):** [Name] – [Phone]
3. **Building Coordinator:** [Name] – [Phone]
4. **Medical Response Team:** [Name] – [Phone]

5. **Emergency Response Team:** [Name] – [Phone]

Night / 24-Hour

1. **Building Maintenance/Trustees:** [Name] – **[24/7 Phone]**
2. **Pastor/Minister(s):** [Name] – **[24/7 Phone]**
3. **Building Coordinator:** [Name] – **[24/7 Phone]**
4. **Medical Response Team:** [Name] – **[24/7 Phone]**
5. **Emergency Response Team:** [Name] – **[24/7 Phone]**

Community Numbers

- **9-1-1** (or local emergency dispatch): [If not 911, list number]
- **Police (non-emergency):** [Number]
- **Fire (non-emergency):** [Number]
- **EMS (non-emergency):** [Number]
- **Poison Control:** 1-800-222-1222 (US)
- **Utility (Gas/Electric/Water):** [Numbers]

Safety Response Team (SRT) – Roles & Duties

Team Members (All)

- Know the notification process; review the Emergency Operations Plan (EOP).
- Know routes, alarms, extinguishers, pull stations, and AEDs.
- Assist evacuations/sheltering; report missing or trapped persons.

Building Coordinator

- Master of floor plans and scenario procedures.
- Receives reports from Incident Coordinator; relays them to fire/police/EMS.
- Coordinates evacuations with responders and supports long-range planning and training.

Incident Coordinator

- Leads on-scene implementation of the EOP until relieved by officials/senior leaders.
- Assigns SRT tasks; maintains comms; ensures 911 call and information flow.

Medical Response Team

- First aid/CPR/AED; primary assessments; care until EMS arrival; handoff reports.

Safety Response Team (by Area/Floor)

- Sweep zones, evacuate, and report "clear" to IC.
- Implement lockdown/shelter-in-place as directed.
- Maintain radios; wear visible ID (vests/badges).

Leader Responsibilities (Quick-Action)

- Call **911** promptly and give the precise location and nature of the emergency.
- Initiate correct protocol (evacuation, lockdown, shelter-in-place).
- Close doors, control utilities if instructed, and coordinate with SRT.

Warning Signs & General Safety Messaging

Concerning Behaviors (Report Immediately)

1. Threats of harm or talk of killing others
2. Frequent fighting/aggression
3. Extreme anger/impulse control problems
4. Persistent vulgar/menacing language with escalating hostility
5. Graphic drawings/writings of death/violence
6. Repeated domestic violence involvement
7. Escalating frustration → uncontrollable physical violence

Action: Document specifics; notify leadership; **contact law enforcement** per policy. Prioritize safety and confidentiality.

Hazard Awareness Briefs (Rotate in Teaching/Signage)

- **Flooding:** Avoid floodways; move to higher ground; never drive through water.
- **HazMat Spills:** Evacuate upwind if instructed; avoid contact; report exact location.
- **Severe Weather:** Know shelter areas; heed alerts.
- **Earthquakes: Drop–Cover–Hold On**; evacuate when safe.
- **Fire:** Know routes; know PASS for extinguishers (Pull, Aim, Squeeze, Sweep).

Appendices (Printable Templates)

Appendix A – Threat Call Checklist (Bomb/Violence/Custody)

- **Time of call:** ____ **Date:** ____
- **Exact words of caller:** ________________________________

- **Voice:** ☐ Male ☐ Female ☐ Adult ☐ Youth Age est: ___

- **Tone (circle):** Calm / Nervous / Angry / Excited / Slurred / Loud / Whisper / Disguised / Accent / Crying / Giggling / Stressed / Nasal / Other: ___
- **If familiar, sounds like:** ________________________________

- **Background noises (circle):** Music / Children / Typing / Aircraft / Machinery / Traffic / Other: ___

Questions to ask (record verbatim):

1. When will it happen? 2) Where is it? 3) What does it look like?
2. What kind is it? 5) Activation method? 6) Deactivation?
3. Did you place it? 8) Why? 9) Where are you calling from?
4. Your address? 11) Your name?

Call received by: __________ **Dept:** ______ **Ext:** ______

Immediate steps:

- Call **911**: "We received a bomb/threat call." Provide location/extension.

- Preserve notes and **do not hang up** until told by authorities. Stay calm.

Appendix B — Evacuation & Shelter Maps (Insert Your Maps)

Instructions to occupants (print on each map):

- Follow marked routes to the **assembly/rally point**.
- Assist those with disabilities.
- Shelter-in-place: proceed to **interior rooms** as marked.
- Remain until the **all-clear**.

Review maps after any renovation or room reassignment.

Appendix C — Outside Triage Area Map

- Proceed to the **designated triage area** when directed.
- Do not re-enter until cleared by officials.
- Medical lead establishes patient tags, treatment zones, and transport lanes.

Appendix D — Rally Points

- Primary & secondary rally points labeled per building.
- Wardens conduct headcounts and report to IC.
- Keep drives clear for responders.

Appendix E — Injury/Incident Report (One-Page Form)

- **Date: ____ Injured person: __________ Completed by: ______**
- **Location at time of injury: ________________________________**
- **Description & how it occurred: _____________________________**
- (Attach photos if applicable.)
- **Witnesses: ____**

- **Actions taken / Treatment provided:**
  ____

- **Reported to (name/role):** ____________ **Time:** _____________

Store securely; share with insurer and only those with a need to know.

Appendix F — Building Emergency Systems (Fill with Site Details)

Fire/Smoke Detection & Warning

- Sprinkler coverage: [Areas]
- Alarms: [Type/sounds/strobes]
- Extinguishers: [Types & map references]
- Emergency lighting: [Locations/tests schedule]

Emergency Power

- Generators/UPS: [Locations, circuits covered, weekly/monthly test plan]

Alarm Recognition Guide

- Signal A (Fire): [tone/flash pattern] — **Evacuate**

- Signal B (Severe Weather): [tone/message] – **Shelter**
- Signal C (Lockdown): [code phrase/tone] – **Secure/Harden**

Quick-Reference: Protective Actions Across a Campus

- **Evacuation:** Two routes per area; rally points; accountability.
- **Sheltering:** Pre-identified interior safe rooms by building.
- **Shelter-in-Place:** Interior upper-floor rooms; seal; shut HVAC.
- **Lockdown:** Lock/barricade, silence, and conceal; Run–Hide–Fight if necessary.
- **Earthquake:** Drop–Cover–Hold On, then staged evacuation after safety check.

"God is our refuge and strength, an ever-present help in trouble."

– Ps. 46:1

www.ingramcontent.com/pod-product-compliance
Ingram Content Group UK Ltd.
Pitfield, Milton Keynes, MK11 3LW, UK
UKHW062313290726
14090UKWH00018B/1036

9 781968 762582